Mrs Cadogan's Cookbook

M^{RS} CADOGAN'S COOKBOOK

RECIPES FOR THE IRISH R.M.

Illustrations by Michael Craig

STANLEY PAUL

London Melbourne Sydney Auckland Johannesburg

Stanley Paul & Co. Ltd

An imprint of the Hutchinson Publishing Group

17–21 Conway Street, London W1P 6JD

Hutchinson Publishing Group (Australia) Pty Ltd
PO Box 496, 16–22 Church Street, Hawthorne, Melbourne, Victoria 3122

Hutchinson Group (NZ) Ltd
32–34 View Road, PO Box 40–086, Glenfield, Auckland 10

Hutchinson Group (SA) Pty Ltd
PO Box 337, Bergvlei 2012, South Africa

First published 1984

Text © Lodge Productions Limited 1984
Illustrations © Michael Craig 1984

Set in Linotron Horley Old Style Light
by Tradespools Ltd, Frome, Somerset

Printed and bound in Great Britain
by Redwood Burn Ltd, Trowbridge, Wiltshire

British Library Cataloguing
in Publication Data

Mrs. Cadogan's cookbook.
1. Cookery, Irish
I. Title
641.59415   TX717.5

ISBN 0 09 158191 5

CONTENTS

The television series *The Irish R.M.* is a James Mitchell production for Channel 4 in association with Rediffusion Films, Ulster Television and RTE.

Peter Bowles stars in *The Irish R.M.* Also starring are Bryan Murray as Flurry Knox, Doran Godwin as Philippa, Lise-Ann McLaughlin as Sally Knox, Anna Manahan as Mrs Cadogan, and Brendan Conroy as Peter Cadogan.

The series is based on the works of Somerville and Ross, adapted for television by Rosemary Anne Sisson.

WEIGHTS AND MEASURES, FACTS AND FIGURES

Notes on metrication

In this book quantities are given in imperial and metric measures. Exact conversions do not usually give very convenient working quantities and so the metric measures have been rounded off into units of 25 grams. The table below shows the recommended equivalents.

Ounces	Approx g to nearest whole figure	Recommended conversion to nearest unit of 25
1	28	25
2	57	50
3	85	75
4	113	100
5	142	150
6	170	175
7	198	200
8	227	225
9	255	250
10	283	275
11	312	300
12	340	350
13	368	375
14	396	400
15	425	425
16 (1 lb)	454	450

LIQUID MEASURES

The millilitre has been used in this book and the following table gives a few examples.

Imperial	*Approx ml to nearest whole figure*	*Recommended ml*
¼ pint	142	150 ml
½ pint	283	300 ml
¾ pint	425	450 ml
1 pint	567	600 ml
1½ pints	851	900 ml
1¾ pints	992	1000 ml (1 litre)

SPOON MEASURES

All spoon measures given in this book are level unless otherwise stated.

OVEN TEMPERATURES

The table below gives recommended equivalents.

	°F	°C	*Gas mark*
Very cool	225	110	¼
	250	120	½
Cool	275	140	1
	300	150	2
Moderate	325	160	3
	350	180	4
Moderately hot	375	190	5
	400	200	6
Hot	425	220	7
	450	230	8
Very hot	475	240	9

Notes for American users

In America the 8-oz measuring cup is used. The Imperial pint, used in Britain and Australia, is 20 fl oz, while the American pint is 16 fl oz. The table below gives a comparison between American and British spoon measures. The British standard tablespoon, which has been used throughout this book, holds 17·7ml, and the American 14·2ml. A teaspoon holds approximately 5ml in both countries.

British	American
1 teaspoon	1 teaspoon
1 tablespoon	1 tablespoon
2 tablespoons	3 tablespoons
3½ tablespoons	4 tablespoons
4 tablespoons	5 tablespoons

An Imperial/American guide to solid and liquid measures

SOLID MEASURES

Imperial	American
1lb butter or margarine	2 cups
1lb flour	4 cups
1lb granulated or caster sugar	2 cups
1lb icing sugar	3 cups
8oz rice	1 cup

LIQUID MEASURES

Imperial	American
¼ pint liquid	⅔ cup liquid
½ pint	1¼ pints
¾ pint	2 cups
1 pint	2½ cups
1½ pints	3¾ cups
2 pints	5 cups (2½ pints)

NOTE: When making any of the recipes in this book, only follow one set of measures as they are not interchangeable.

——————————————EQUIPMENT AND TERMS——————————————

The list below gives some American equivalents or substitutes for terms and ingredients used in the text.

English	*American*
Absorbent paper	Absorbent paper
Baking/roasting tin	Baking/roasting pan
Baking tray	Baking/cookie sheet
Deep cake tin	Springform pan
Double saucepan	Double boiler
Flan tin	Pie tin
Fricassée	Fricassee
Frying pan	Skillet
Greaseproof paper	Waxed paper
Grill/grilled	Broil/broiled
Gut fish	Clean fish
Minced	Ground
Mix/liquidise	Mix/blend
Muslin	Cheesecloth
Packet	Package
Pipe, using a plain nozzle in a piping bag	Pipe, using a fluted nozzle or tip in a pastry bag
Prove dough	Rise dough
Stoned	Pitted
Whip cream	Whip cream
Whisk eggs	Beat eggs

————————————————INGREDIENTS————————————————

Apple, cooking	Apple, baking
Aubergine	Eggplant
Bacon rashers	Bacon slices
Beef suet, shredded	Beef suet, chopped
Belly of pork	Salt pork
Bicarbonate of soda	Baking soda
Biscuits	Crackers or cookies
Boiling chicken/fowl	Stewing chicken
Broad beans	Fava or Lima beans
1 cabbage, lettuce	1 head cabbage, lettuce
Cake mixture	Cake batter
Celery stick	Celery stalk
Chocolate, cooking	Unsweetened chocolate squares

English	*American*
Chocolate, plain	Chocolate, semi-sweet
Cocoa powder	Unsweetened cocoa
Confectioner's custard	Pastry cream
Cornflour	Cornstarch
Courgettes	Zucchini
Cream, single	Cream, light
Cream, double	Cream, heavy
Cream, soured	Cream, dairy sour
Crystallized and glacé fruits	Candied fruits
Dripping	Drippings
Essence	Extract
Flour, plain	Flour, all-purpose
Flour, self-raising	Flour, all-purpose sifted with baking powder
Fresh white breadcrumbs	Fresh soft breadcrumbs
Freshly opened oysters	Freshly shucked oysters
Fresh yeast	Compressed yeast
Gammon steak	Bacon or ham steak
Gingernuts	Gingersnaps
hard-boiled eggs	Hard-cooked eggs
Icing	Frosting
Lamb, best end of neck	Rack of lamb or rib roast
Paprika	Paprika pepper
Shortcrust pastry	Basic pie dough
Shrimps or prawns	Shrimp
Spring onion	Scallion
Stock cube	Bouillon cube
Sugar, caster	Superfine
Sugar, granulated	Granulated
Sugar, icing	Confectioner's
Sugar, demerara	Light brown
Sultanas	Seedless white raisins
Tomato purée	Tomato paste
Vanilla pod	Vanilla bean
Veal escallopes	Veal scallops
Whiskey	Whisky
Yeast, fresh	Yeast, compressed
Yeast, dried	Yeast, dry active
Yoghurt, natural	Yogurt, plain

FOREWORD

BY ROSEMARY ANNE SISSON

The first meeting between Major Sinclair Yeates and Mrs Cadogan is one of those classic encounters in literature, like Antony surveying Cleopatra on her barge, or Romeo catching sight of Juliet across a crowded ballroom. This particular meeting was not quite so romantic, but still it began a relationship of lasting fascination, and – like all the best relationships – never entirely predictable.

It was, according to Major Yeates, a wet and windy day in October when he stood on the steps of Shreelane House, waiting for the door to be opened, while the rain sluiced down upon him from a broken eaveshoot. When the door opened, he perceived 'a large elderly woman with a red face and a cap worn helmet-wise on her forehead.'

'"Your honour's welcome –" she began, and then every door in the house slammed in obedience to the gust that drove through it. With something like "Mend ye for a back door!" Mrs Cadogan abandoned her opening speech and made for the kitchen stairs. (Improbable as it may appear, my housekeeper was called Cadogan, a name made locally possible by being pronounced Caydogawn.)'

What kind of cook is Mrs Cadogan? Major Yeates speaks of 'the surprises' of her cooking, and clearly she triumphs in an emergency, an Irish characteristic, and just as well, too, since her kitchen would hardly have satisfied Mrs Beeton or even Mrs Bridges. It is lit by candlelight, the rat-holes are plugged up with biscuit-boxes, and, although the kitchen stove is never precisely described, the Sweep is able to take 'three ass-loads of soot' from the chimney before the draught is such that it would 'dhraw up a young cat with it!' And when the meal is over, the dishes are washed in a pantry sink which, when it gets blocked up, as inevitably it does, is bitterly described by Mrs Cadogan to the Major's landlord, the insouciant Flurry Knox, as 'that unnatural little trough.'

In this unpromising venue does Mrs Cadogan produce her culinary triumphs.

'Never, while Mrs Cadogan can hold a basting-spoon, will she cease to recount how she plucked and roasted ten couple of woodcock in one torrid hour to provide luncheon for the hunt.'

Clearly, she is not dismayed by the arrival of the present of 'a fine young goose' from Bat Callaghan's mother, and a similar unwanted bribe of live lobsters, though an embarrassment to the Resident Magistrate, is presumably dealt with in the course of time by his cook. However, although she may be prepared to fry herrings with onions, she 'will not go to them extremes for servants.'

Major Yeates' wife, Philippa, possesses an unappeasable appetite for picnics, in which unholy enthusiasm she is aided and abetted by Mrs Cadogan, even if 'a moist chicken pie' is the outcome. When Philippa indulges in her other passion, that of unbridled hospitality at the Peter and Paul's Day Games, Mrs Cadogan is to be found outside the crowded tea-tent devotedly striving, as she says, 'to keep the kettle simpering on the fire, and not as much coals undher it as'd redden a pipe!' She certainly cannot be accused of prodigality. When Maria, Philippa's Irish water spaniel, takes hold of the roast beef which has emerged from the dining-room and which Mrs Cadogan had planned for next day's luncheon, 'the way we wouldn't have to inthrude on the cold turkey,' she is instantly inspired instead to 'run the remains of the beef through the mincing machine for the Major's sandwiches.'

In the Somerville and Ross stories, the only account of a formal dinner-party cooked by Mrs Cadogan is given in the story 'The Boat's Share'. The menu appears to consist of soup, initially prepared by means of an indeterminate head and feet 'boiling in the pot', followed by pollock rashly bought at the door by the Major from the kitchen-maid's mother, Mrs Brickley.

'Sha' thim's not company fish!' says Mrs Cadogan, contemptuously.

By an unfortunate chance, the sleeve of Philippa's best dress is taken to strain the soup by the accident-prone kitchen-maid, Bridget, who, in the subsequent *fracas*, retires to bed in hysterics. Mrs Cadogan, 'in an ecstasy of achievement,' copes single-handed with the emergency, and Major Yeates, having presumably performed his duties of 'getting out the champagne and reverentially decanting the port,' describes the soup as being 'of a transparency that did infinite credit to Philippa's sleeve,' and the pollock as having emerged 'chastely robed in white sauce.'

The main dish for this dinner-party is not particularized, but, drawing on evidence elsewhere in the stories, it could have been roast saddle of mutton or cutlets, or possibly duck, with an open tart to follow. (Philippa's menu-slate would hardly have admitted sago on such an occasion.) We may be sure that Mrs Cadogan is a mistress of the ubiquitous Irish dish of boiled turkey and ham and that a fresh salmon or lake trout is safer in her hands than in those of her enemy, Maggie Nolan of Aussolas Castle.

At all times of crisis or comedy in Shreelane House, Mrs Cadogan is there, putting breakfast, luncheon, tea or dinner before the Resident Magistrate, his family and guests – not to mention the more mysterious provender consumed round the kitchen table. (Did she, one asks oneself, ever serve up drisheen?) Mere loyalty compels us to assume that Mrs Cadogan's barm brack is the best in the country, and that her potato cakes, swimming in butter, are superior to all others.

In short, those of us who know and love Ireland – and *The Irish R.M.* – can well imagine that combination of thrift, simplicity, generosity and inspired improvisation which will find its triumphant apotheosis in Mrs Cadogan's kitchen.

Rosemary Anne Sisson

WHO'S WHO IN
THE IRISH R.M.

Major Sinclair Yeates, a retired army officer, came to the West of Ireland to take up the arduous post of Resident Magistrate. Like many features of an earlier regime, the post is no more, and its incumbents 'no longer vie with the snipe and dispensary doctor in endurance of conditions which test even those exponents of the art of being jolly in creditable circumstances'. The Major went from courthouse to courthouse supposedly imparting a dispassionate flavour to local justice, although he was equipped only 'with a feeling heart, and the belief that two and two inevitably makes four, whereas in Ireland they are just as likely to make five, or three, and are still more likely to make nothing at all'. He learned endurance, developed a sense of humour that had almost been stifled by the stuffy atmosphere of the Officers' Mess, and mastered the fine shades of definition that separate offences in Ireland. A man might have 'drink taken' and be 'a contrary little man and never duly sober' while 'swearing unearthly oaths' but the prosecuting police sergeant would offer the extenuating fact that 'it was all that was the matter with him he had no sense'.

The Major went to live at Shreelane House, Skebawn, tall and ugly from the outside, cold and damp from the inside. Until he was joined by his wife philippa, a soothing female presence, he was eccentrically ministered to by Mrs Cadogan and her nephew Peter. The Major awoke on his first morning at Shreelane to find Peter Cadogan standing by his bedside. He asked the lad to run him a bath. 'There is no bath in the house, sir', was his reply to the command, 'but me aunt said would you like a taggeen'. This alternative proved to be a glass of raw whiskey. He declined it.

His landlord was Mr Florence McCarthy Knox, better known as Flurry. 'A stable boy among gentlemen and a gentleman among stable boys', Flurry Knox was prepared at any moment of day or night to sell a horse. He occupied a shifting position about mid-way up the ranks of the ubiquitous Knox tribe, a clan that 'cropped up in every grade of society from Sir Valentine Knox of Castle Knox down to the auctioneer Knox who bore the attractive title of Larry the Liar'. Flurry's grandmother and sparring partner was the redoubtable Mrs Knox, who lived in the fascinating chaos of Aussolas Castle and whose attire could be summarized by saying that she looked as if she had robbed a scarecrow.

Flurry eventually managed to combine in the person of Sally Knox a cousin and a wife. As Major Yeates and Flurry formed strong bonds of affection and mutual misunderstanding that characterize Anglo-Irish relations, so Philippa Yeates and Sally soon became intimates and champions of Flurry's sometimes beleaguered cause. Flurry's misdemeanours often caught the disapproving eye of Sally's mother Lady Knox, 'an eye decisive from long habit of taking her own line across country and elsewhere'. Flurry's most effective ally was the egregious and omniscient Slipper, who had an eye like a profligate pug and, with his rolling gait, was never far behind the jaunty stride of his young master.

Skebawn life was often enriched by appearances from many other great characters, several of whom have provided the inspiration for some of Mrs Cadogan's greatest dishes. Those who have stimulated the red-faced genius, her cap worn helmet-wise on her forehead, to culinary achievement merit a brief mention.

MISS BOBBY BENNETT: A handsome horsewoman from Curranhilty Country, especially admired by Major Yeates. Combining elegance with toughness, she elicited a great compliment from Flurry to the effect that 'you couldn't hurt that one unless you took a hatchet to her'.

BRIDGIE BRICKLEY: Bridget Brickley, assistant to Mrs Cadogan in the kitchen, who became the wife of Peter Cadogan, giving rise to speculation on the results of an extraordinary genetic adventure.

MRS BRICKLEY: Mother of the Shreelane kitchen-maid Bridget Brickley, and purveyor of fish. Mrs Brickley, in looks akin to Deborah the prophetess, attempted to sell the Major a pollock upon which her cat had previously feasted.

THE WIDOW CALLAGHAN: Matriarchal leader of the Callaghan family, implacable enemies of the Foley clan. The Widow Callaghan successfully attempted to prejudice Major Yeates' judgement with the gift of a goose, from which Mrs Cadogan created a classic pâté.

MRS CANTY: Wife of farmer James Canty, a noted member of the Skebawn Board of Guardians and bassoon-like basso profundo in Philippa Yeates' Glee Club. Mrs Canty's Oatmeal Herrings were famous throughout the West of Ireland.

CHICHESTER: A friend from Philippa's past and, as such, treated by Major Yeates with great suspicion. A veritable gourmet, he found it difficult to start the day without a Breakfast Oatcake.

MRS COFFEY: Proprietress of a famous fish emporium in Carrig Junction. Renowned for the soft flesh of her fish and the hard strike of her bargain.

JOHN CULLINANE: Best known for his gullibility in purchasing undesirable horses. A dealer's delight.

TOMSY FLOOD: A huge eater who had a particular weakness for chocolates. Unfortunately he later developed a partiality for spirits and went to work on a South African ostrich farm.

DR HICKEY: The dispensary doctor in Skebawn and whipper-in for Flurry's hunt. Opinions were divided as to which office was the more important. Of fine appearance, Dr Hickey was considered something of a lady's man.

SIR VALENTINE KNOX: Quiet and self-effacing husband of Lady Knox, affectionate father of Sally Knox. The former sometimes gave him cause to rue the day he had been born, the latter often gave him cause to bless the day she had been.

LARRY THE LIAR: Another member of the Knox family, although most Knoxes attempted to deny it. He was a famed auctioneer who, it was widely believed, could find a buyer for the holes in a bucket.

BASIL LEIGH KELWAY: A university colleague of Major Yeates, he attempted a doomed study of the Liquor Question in Ireland for the British Government, which started in Mahona (a village boasting fifteen public houses out of twenty buildings) and ended in a ditch.

MAGGIE NOLAN: A great rival of Mrs Cadogan, Maggie Nolan was the cook at Aussolas Castle. She was famous for consistent production of burnt food caused by her bad sense of time rather than her chosen ingredients.

MRS O'FEE: A job cook who came to Shreelane when Mrs Cadogan went to a family wake. She 'tasted' too much of the Major's wine and spent the night in the pantry.

THE COMTE DE PRALINE: As an extravagant jest, Mr John Simpson-Hodges hunted with the Curranhilty Hunt under the assumed name of The Comte de Praline. His faultless French accent and identity completely disappeared in the excitement of the chase.

ROARING JACK: The 'trade' name of that most widely heard and deeply respected solicitor, Mr John Mooney.

WIDOW TWOHIG: Highly voluble mother of Oweneen The Sprat, a mischievous mountain-dweller who attempted to extort money from Major Yeates by pinning dried sprats on the door of Shreelane House.

BREAKFAST

Major Yeates' Ideal Breakfast

————————————INGREDIENTS————————————

1 sea trout	1 oz (25 g) butter
2 rashers back bacon	1 tomato
2 slices white bread	salt and pepper

————————————METHOD————————————

Clean and dry a small sea trout (no bigger than 2 lb (1 kg)). Wrap the fish in a rasher of bacon and put on a rack inside a roasting tin. Cook in a hot oven, 400°F (200°C, gas mark 6) for 20 minutes. Serve hot, with an extra rasher of bacon, cut in strips and crisply fried, the slices of bread fried in butter and cut into triangles, and slices of tomato. *Serves 4.*

Irish Stirabout and Oatmeal Bread

To create oatmeal bread it is necessary to start by making Irish stirabout (porridge). This is a meal in itself and has been described as 'the treasure that is smoothest and sweetest of all foods'.

————————————INGREDIENTS————————————

5 oz (150 g) oatmeal	1 teaspoon sugar
1½ pints (900 ml) boiling water	

————————————METHOD————————————

Sprinkle the oatmeal into the boiling water, stirring all the time. Boil for 5 minutes and then cover and simmer for 15 minutes, adding the sugar near the end. From this amount of Stirabout extract ½ pint (300 ml) for the Oatmeal Bread (see p. 22). *Serves 6.*

Oatmeal Bread

---INGREDIENTS---

½ pint (300 ml) Stirabout   1½ lb (¾ kg) wholemeal flour
  (see above)   ½ oz (15 g) fresh yeast
1 oz (25 g) butter   ½ pint (300 ml) tepid milk
1 tablespoon treacle   1 teaspoon salt

---METHOD---

Add the butter, treacle and salt to the Stirabout. Make a well in the centre of the flour and fill it with the porridge mixture. Soften the yeast in the tepid milk and stir this into the porridge. Leave it in a warm place overnight, knead well the next morning and allow the dough to stand for another hour. Grease two 1-lb (450-g) tins and bake in a moderate oven, 350°F (180°C, gas mark 4) for 40 minutes.

Mrs Canty's Oatmeal Herring

The first time Major Yeates tasted Mrs Canty's oatmeal herring, he was so transported with joy by the excellence of the fish, and so carried away by a glass or two of whiskey, that he decided to tell Mrs Canty this joke. The joke was not a very good one, nor did Mrs Canty understand it, but she remembered it because she respected his honour, Major Yeates.

Two herrings are together in a school of fish. One says to the other, 'I must tell you, I am not my brother's kipper.'

---INGREDIENTS---

4 herrings   oz (2 g) 50 oz (butter
salt   chopped parsley
¼ pint (150 ml) milk   1 lemon
2 oz (50 g) oatmeal

---METHOD---

Gut the herrings and wash them in cold, salted water. Dip each herring in milk and roll in oatmeal. Heat up the butter and fry the oatmealed herrings for 5 minutes on each side. Serve with parsley and lemon wedges. *Serves 3 to 4.*

Chichester's Breakfast Oatcakes

'Chichester was an elderly young man, worn smooth by much visiting in country houses, and thoroughly competent in the avocations proper to his career. If you gave him a map he could put a pudgy finger upon the good cooks as promptly as an archbishop upon his cathedral towns; to see his eye, critical, yet alight with healthful voracity, travelling down the array of dishes on the sidetable at breakfast, and arranging unhesitatingly the order in which they' were to be attended, was a lesson to the heedless who blunt the fine edge of appetite with porridge.'

Some Experiences of an Irish R.M.

———————————————INGREDIENTS———————————————

4 tablespoons flour	1 egg, beaten
3 tablespoons oatmeal	1 teaspoon baking powder
a little milk	butter and oil
salt and pepper	

———————————————METHOD———————————————

Steep overnight the flour and oatmeal in sufficient milk to make a thick batter, with salt and pepper to taste. Next morning add the beaten egg and baking powder and mix well. Shape into small round cakes and fry in a mixture of butter and oil or in beef dripping. This is superb with rashers as a breakfast dish. *Makes about 6.*

Kidneys in their Overcoats

Major Yeates liked nothing better than three or four kidneys on toast for breakfast before setting out to take assizes.

———————————————INGREDIENTS———————————————

For each serving:	1 slice fresh toast
4 lambs' kidneys	salt and pepper

———————————————METHOD———————————————

Put the kidneys, encased in their overcoats of fat, into a preheated oven, 400°F (200°C, gas mark 6). Leave for 30 minutes or until the fat is melted. Break the kidneys open, place them on the toast and season with salt and pepper.

Mrs Cadogan's Kedgeree

---------------------------------INGREDIENTS---------------------------------

1 lb (450 g) smoked haddock fillets	4 oz (100 g) rice
2 eggs	1 teaspoon cayenne pepper
1 medium onion	salt and pepper
2 oz (50 g) butter	chopped parsley

---------------------------------METHOD---------------------------------

Pour boiling water over the haddock fillets, then drain them after a few minutes. Remove the skin and divide into pieces. Hard-boil the eggs, and chop them.

Chop the onion and soften it in half the butter. Boil the rice until just tender, drain and add to the onions in the pan, with the cayenne pepper, salt and pepper. Stir over a moderate heat until hot all through, then turn into a serving dish and top with the chopped eggs and parsley and the rest of the butter, cut in pieces. *Serves 4.*

Skebawn Fishcakes

---------------------------------INGREDIENTS---------------------------------

1 lb (450 g) cooked white fish	½ pint (300 ml) milk
1½ tablespoons chopped parsley	1 egg yolk
2½–3 oz (65–70 g) fresh	1 teaspoon anchovy essence
breadcrumbs	salt and pepper
1 oz (25 g) flour	1 egg, beaten
1 oz (25 g) butter	cooking oil

---------------------------------METHOD---------------------------------

Flake the fish and mix in the parsley and 1 oz (25 g) of the breadcrumbs. Blend the flour, butter and milk together in a saucepan and cook for 2 minutes. Take the mixture off the heat and stir in the egg yolk. Add the anchovy essence, pepper and salt. Amalgamate this with the fish mixture and chill it. Form the mixture into cakes, using floured hands. Dip first in beaten egg and then in breadcrumbs. Heat the oil and fry for about 5 minutes on each side. *Serves 4.*

Mrs Canty's Potato Cakes

'While I live I shall not forget her potato cakes. They came in hot and hot from a pot-oven, they were speckled with caraway seeds, they swam in salt butter, and we ate them shamelessly and greasily, and washed them down with hot whisky and water'.

Some Experiences of an Irish R.M.

——————————————INGREDIENTS——————————————

1 oz (25 g) butter   1 teaspoon salt
8 oz (225 g) cold mashed potatoes   3 oz (75 g) flour

——————————————METHOD——————————————

Melt the butter and mix it with the mashed potatoes. Add salt and work the flour in to make a paste. Roll out into a thin sheet, cut out squares or desired shapes and put on a hot griddle for 3 minutes on each side. Serve hot with butter or, best of all, with bacon.

FIRST COURSES

Mrs Cadogan's Cold Cucumber Soup

INGREDIENTS

1 large cucumber
½ pint (300 ml) single cream
¼ pint (150 ml) natural yoghurt
1½ tablespoons tarragon vinegar

1 clove crushed garlic
salt and pepper
2 tablespoons chopped mint

METHOD

Peel the cucumber and grate it into a tureen. Stir in all the other ingredients except for the mint which should be added just before serving. Chill. *Serves 4.*

Doctor Hickey's Watercress Soup

INGREDIENTS

2 oz (50 g) butter
2 medium potatoes
2 medium onions
salt and pepper
1 pint (600 ml) water

8 oz (225 g) watercress
1½ pints (900 ml) milk
4 tablespoons double cream
1 egg yolk

METHOD

Melt the butter in a saucepan and add the potatoes and onions, chopped small. Turn the vegetables in the butter and season. Cover the saucepan and gently cook the buttered vegetables for 10 minutes. Meanwhile heat up the water and add the watercress, chopped, followed by the potatoes and onions. Simmer until the vegetables are just soft. Liquidize in a blender or put through a sieve, return to a clean saucepan and reheat. Season. Shortly before serving add the milk and beat in the cream mixed with the egg yolk and heat through. The liquid must not boil again or the yolk will curdle. Serve in individual bowls with a watercress leaf as a garnish. *Serves 6.*

Maggie Nolan's Cream Cheese and Tomato Soup

————————————————INGREDIENTS————————————————

2 oz (50 g) butter	¾ pint (450 ml) chicken stock
1 onion	salt and pepper
1 clove garlic	2 tablespoons tomato purée
1 14-oz (397-g) can tomatoes	2 oz (50 g) noodles
1 teaspoon sugar	4 oz (100 g) cream cheese

————————————————METHOD————————————————

Melt the butter in a saucepan. Slice the onion, crush the garlic and fry together for 5 minutes. Add the canned tomatoes, sugar, stock, seasoning, 1 pint (600 ml) water and tomato purée. Bring to the boil and simmer, covered, for 30 minutes. Add the noodles and simmer for a further 8 minutes. Stir the soup to separate the pasta. Add in the cream cheese, little by little, and stir over the heat until dissolved. Serve immediately. *Serves 4.*

Fisherman's Soup

If a fisherman in Ireland wishes to be successful he must obey the old customs of the country. If he doesn't, surely he will catch nothing.

While fishing at sea he must never mention a priest, a pig or a weasel. Three men of the same Christian name must never fish together.

Fishermen must not smoke while at work.

A fisherman's wife must throw a live coal from the fire after him as he leaves the house for his day's work.

─────────────────────────INGREDIENTS─────────────────────────

2 onions	1 handful parsley, chopped
2 carrots	1 bay leaf
2 potatoes	1 teaspoon chopped thyme
1 oz (25 g) butter	1 pint (600 ml) milk
2 lb (1 kg) smoked haddock fillets	grated nutmeg

─────────────────────────METHOD─────────────────────────

Chop the vegetables and simmer them in the butter until soft. Add the fish, skinned and cut in pieces, and the herbs and continue to simmer until both the vegetables and fish are cooked. Add the milk and 2 pints (1·2 litres), water. Simmer for 10 minutes and grate nutmeg into it just before serving. *Serves 6.*

Beautiful Head and Lovely Feet Soup

'All was peace. Peace, I say, but even as I expanded in it and the sunshine, there arose to me the voice of Mrs Cadogan, uplifted in passionate questioning.

'"Bridgie", it wailed. "Where's me beautiful head and me lovely feet?".

'The answer to this amazing enquiry came shrilly from the region of the scullery.

'"Bilin' in the pot, ma'am". I realized that it was merely soup in its elemental stage that was under discussion, but Peace spread her wings at the cry; it recalled the fact that Philippa was having a dinner party that same night.'
                                                    Further Experiences of an Irish R.M.

─────────────────────────INGREDIENTS─────────────────────────

carcasses and trimmings of 2 game birds and about 8 oz (225 g) pieces of breast	1 onion
	1 carrot
	1 parsnip
2 oz (50 g) chopped bacon	1 stick celery
1 oz (25 g) butter	1 clove
1 oz (25 g) flour	salt and pepper
2 pints (1 litre) game stock	

─────────────────────────METHOD─────────────────────────

Fry the carcasses, trimmings, breast meat and bacon in the butter in a saucepan until they are brown. Add the flour, frying it until golden brown. Stir in the stock and bring to the boil. Chop the vegetables.

Remove the game from the pan and add the vegetables in its place, with the clove. Simmer the liquid for a further 1½ hours. Then strain the soup and return the breast meat, diced into ¼-inch (·5-cm) pieces. Reheat, season and serve. *Serves 4.*

Scallop Soup

---INGREDIENTS---

8 oz (225 g) potatoes	8 large scallops
2 oz (50 g) butter	salt and pepper
1 teaspoon chopped fresh thyme	6 tomatoes
2 tablespoons chopped parsley	2½ fl oz (75 ml) cream
1 pint (600 ml) fish stock (see page 109)	

---METHOD---

Dice the potatoes and sauté them in a saucepan in the butter. Add the thyme and half the parsley, with the fish stock. Bring to the boil and simmer for 20 minutes before adding blanched and diced scallops. Simmer for 15 minutes and add salt and pepper to taste. Then add the tomatoes, peeled and diced, to the soup. Pour into a tureen, and stir in the cream and the remaining chopped parsley. *Serves 4.*

Fortune and Potato Soup

Mrs Cadogan, like many of her kind, was a superstitious woman. She took many precautions to ensure that fortune smiled on Shreelane and its inhabitants.

She always kept one raw leek in the kitchen: this prevented the house from ever burning down. She persuaded Major Yeates to plant an elder tree in the garden: this would protect the house from lightning.

The black cat and black cockerel that roamed around the Shreelane yard both served a purpose. The former ensured luck for the house, the latter protected the house from sorcery or the 'little people'.

The house was never swept on a Monday. Mrs Cadogan said tht if you sweep out the dust on a Monday, you also sweep out your luck.

———————————————INGREDIENTS———————————————

6 leeks   1½ pints (900 ml) hot milk
2 tablespoons butter   4 tablespoons double cream
2 teaspoons salt   pepper
8 potatoes   1 tablespoon chopped parsley

———————————————METHOD———————————————

Clean the leeks and chop them small, then melt the butter in a pan and sauté them until they are soft. Add 1 pint (600 ml) water and the salt. Peel and chop the potatoes into small pieces and add them in. Cook for 1 hour, simmering gently with the lid on. Add the heated milk and then sieve the soup. Season and serve with the cream and parsley stirred through. *Serves 6.*

Larry The Liar's Eel Soup

———————————————INGREDIENTS———————————————

2 leeks, sliced   8 oz (225 g) chopped lettuce
1 onion, sliced   ½ pint (300 ml) double cream
2 oz (50 g) butter   3 egg yolks
12 small eels   salt and pepper
8 oz (225 g) chopped spinach   chopped fennel and dill

———————————————METHOD———————————————

Gently fry the leeks and onion in the butter for 5 minutes or so. Add the eels and fry for a further 5 minutes. Add 3 pints (1·8 litres) water, bring to the boil and simmer for 30 minutes. Take the eels from the water, remove their skin and bones and chop them into small cubes. Strain the cooking liquid before adding back the eels; put in the spinach and lettuce. Cook very slowly for 10 minutes. Mix together the cream and egg yolks and add to the soup, stirring all the time. Heat through without allowing to come to the boil again and, just before serving, season and sprinkle with chopped dill and fennel. *Serves 6.*

Mrs Brickley's Pollock Soup

'I called down the area and asked Mrs Cadogan if she wanted fish.

"What fish is it, sir?" replied Mrs Cadogan, presenting at the kitchen window a face like a harvest moon.

"'Tis pollock, ma'am!" shouted Mrs Brickley from the foot of the steps.

"Sha! thim's no good to us!" responded the harvest moon in bitter scorn. "Thim's not company fish!"'

Further Experiences of an Irish R.M.

Mrs Cadogan was not wrong in her judgement of the pollock. The only way to make the poor fish into a delicious dish is to create a soup around it.

--------------------INGREDIENTS--------------------

10 oz (275 g) pollock
1 pint (600 ml) fish stock (page 109)
1 pint (600 ml) milk
1 onion, chopped

2 parsnips, chopped
salt and pepper
lemon juice

--------------------METHOD--------------------

Skin and bone the fish and cut it up. (You can use the skin and bones for stock.) Put all the other ingredients, save the lemon juice, into a saucepan and bring to the boil. Simmer for 20 minutes. Just before serving check the seasoning and add lemon juice to taste. *Serves 4–6.*

The R.M's Oyster Soup

To eat food and to read about food were two of the loves of Major Yeates' life. One of his favourite dishes was oyster soup. While it slipped delicately down, the Major would ruminate about what some of his favourite authors had written about the oyster.

In the beginning, the history of the relationship between man and the oyster was one of ignorance and poverty. In the seventeenth century, Robert Fuller wrote 'he was a very valiant man who first adventured on the eating of oysters'. Sam Weller observed in Charles Dickens' *Pickwick Papers* that 'oysters and poverty seem always to go together.' The great Doctor Johnson was so ashamed to be seen buying oysters that he was forced to 'slip out to buy his cat some oysters, so that his negro servant would not take it out on the cat'. One great Irishman, Dean Swift, even reported that men 'say that oysters are a cruel meat because we eat them alive, then they are uncharitable meat for we leave nothing to the poor, and they are ungodly meat because we never say Grace.'

Man, however, soon learned to love and respect the oyster. In France, 'oysters became the usual opening to a winter breakfast, indeed they were almost indispensable'. One of W.S. Gilbert's characters sang lustily that 'he had often eaten oysters but had never had enough'. The Major found the essence of his thinking on oysters echoed by Saki; he wrote – 'oysters are more beautiful than any religion. There's nothing in Christianity or Buddhism that quite matches the sympathetic unselfishness of the oyster'.

────────────────────INGREDIENTS────────────────────

2 large potatoes	bouquet garni
1 pint (600 ml) milk	salt and pepper
1 dozen fresh oysters	½ oz (15 g) butter
4 oz (100 g) pork belly	

────────────────────METHOD────────────────────

Peel and boil the potatoes and heat the milk. Open the oysters and put them and their liquor in a bowl. Dice the pork belly and fry it over a moderate heat until cooked through, about 8 minutes. Drain and mash the potatoes in a saucepan, adding hot milk gradually. Add the bouquet garni, salt and pepper and bring the mixture to the boil. When it boils, add the pork, the oysters and their liquor and simmer very gently for 3 minutes. Check seasoning and stir in the enrichment butter. *Serves 4.*

Sleeve Soup

'I was tying my tie when my wife's voice summoned me to her room in tones that presaged disaster. Philippa was standing erect, in a white and glittering garment. Her eyes shone, her cheeks glowed. It is not given to everyone to look their best when they are angry, but it undoubtedly is becoming to Philippa.

'"I ask you to look at my dress", she said in a level voice.

'"It looks very nice –", I said cautiously, knowing there was a trap somewhere. "I know it, don't I?"

'"Know it!" replied Philippa witheringly, "did you know that it had only one sleeve?"
She extended her arms; from one depended vague and transparent films of whiteness, the other was bare to the shoulder. I rather prefered it of the two.
'"Well, I can't say I did", I said helplessly, "is that a new fashion?"
There was a spectral knock at the door, and Hannah, the housemaid, slid into the room, purple of face, abject of mien.
'"It's what they're afther tellin' me, ma'am", she panted.
'"T'was took to strain the soup!"
'"They took my sleeve to strain the soup!" repeated Philippa, in a crystal clarity of wrath.'

Further Experiences of an Irish R.M.

————————————INGREDIENTS————————————

2 oz (50 g) pearl barley
1 oz (25 g) butter
1 small carrot, chopped
1 small onion, chopped
1 stick celery, chopped

2 pints (1 litre) stock (page 109)
1 egg
½ pint (300 ml) milk
salt and pepper

————————————METHOD————————————

Wash the barley, put into ¼ pint (150 ml) water and bring to the boil, then strain. Melt the butter and cook the prepared vegetables for a few minutes, keeping the lid on the pan and shaking it occasionally. Add the barley and stock and simmer for 2 hours. Strain. Add the egg and milk beaten together. Reheat slowly, but do not boil. Season and serve hot. *Serves 6.*

Pancake Cohullen

————————————INGREDIENTS————————————

Pancake batter
4 oz (100 g) plain flour
2 eggs
pinch of salt
8 fl oz (250 ml) milk

2 oz (50 g) butter
1 shallot

3 oz (75 g) mushrooms
8 oz (225 g) cooked shrimps
8 oz (225 g) cooked Dublin Bay
        prawns
½ glass Irish whiskey
2 tablespoons single cream
2 oz (50 g) grated cheese

———————————————————————METHOD———————————————————————

First prepare the pancake batter. Sieve the flour into a bowl. Make a well in the middle and break the eggs into it. Add the salt and milk and whisk to a smooth batter. Leave to rest for an hour. Make 8 pancakes: brush a small frying pan with a little butter or oil and cook small, thin pancakes. Pile them on a plate as they are ready.

Melt half the butter in a saucepan. Finely chop the shallot, slice the mushrooms and add to it, with the shrimps, prawns and the Irish whiskey. Add the cream and simmer for 2 minutes. Fill the pancakes with this mixture and fold up. Sprinkle with cheese and dot with the rest of the butter. Brown under a hot grill. *Serves 4.*

The Royal Hotel's Baked Scallops

———————————————————INGREDIENTS———————————————————

12 large scallops	1½ oz (40 g) fresh breadcrumbs
1½ oz (40 g) butter	salt and pepper
1 shallot, finely chopped	2 tablespoons grated cheese
2 tablespoons chopped parsley	juice of ½ lemon

———————————————————————METHOD———————————————————————

Remove the scallops from their shells, slice them and clean 4 of the shells thoroughly. Melt 1 oz (25 g) of the butter in a small pan, gently sauté the shallot till soft, add the sliced scallops and cook briefly – about 3 minutes. Add the parsley and half the breadcrumbs, season and stir through. Put this mixture back into the 4 scallop shells, sprinkle with the rest of the breadcrumbs and the grated cheese, dot with the rest of the butter, squeeze on some lemon juice. Bake in a hot oven, 400°F (200°C, gas mark 6) for 20 minutes. *Serves 4.*

The Widow Callaghan's Goose Pâté

'Mrs Cadogan advanced upon us with the information that the Widow Callaghan from Cluin would be thankful to speak to me, and had brought me a present of a fine young goose ...'

Some Experiences of an Irish R.M.

─────────────────────────INGREDIENTS─────────────────────────

1 lb (450 g) goose flesh	salt and pepper
8 oz (225 g)) belly pork	6 crushed juniper berries
8 oz (225 g) veal	3 tablespoons brandy
2 cloves garlic	¼ pint (150 ml) dry cider
pinch of nutmeg	8 oz (225 g) lean, thin bacon rashers

───────────────────────────METHOD───────────────────────────

Mince, together, the goose flesh, pork and veal. Thoroughly mix. Crush the garlic and add in, with the nutmeg, salt and pepper, juniper berries and brandy. Moisten with cider to make a soft mixture. Line a terrine with rindless rashers and fill up with the pâté mixture. Cover with foil or a lid. Place the dish in a pan half filled with hot water and cook in a slow oven, 300°F (150°C, gas mark 3) until the pâté comes away from the sides, for at least 1½ hours. Remove from the oven, put a weight on top of the pâté, and leave to cool until the next day. *Serves 8 to 10.*

This pâté is also good when made with duck, or chicken instead of goose.

Skebawn Snails

Snails are a delicious treat, a worthy beginning to the finest meal. It took Major Yeates some time to persuade Mrs Cadogan of this, but after considerable initial reluctance, she became almost as enthusiastic as the Major.

The Major's enthusiasm for snails originated from a short holiday in Northern France. There he had first sampled the unequalled delight of the 'escargot'. He decided that one day he would grow his own snails in his own garden.

On his arrival in Ireland, one of the many things that surprised the Major was the number of holes in the cabbage set before him. The culprit, it seemed, was the snail.

So one sunny afternoon, when he was confident that Flurry Knox was not around to mock him, the Major and Peter Cadogan went on a snail hunt. At the end of the afternoon Peter dug a trench around a small area of land. He filled the trench with water and put the snails on the land. The Major therefore had a snail farm and could look forward to eating cabbage less full of holes.

All snails are edible. The only precaution you must take, as the Major well knew, is to ensure that your snails have been eating nothing unwholesome. When he had singled out a suitable number of snails from their island paradise, the Major would put them under a flower pot for a week, feeding them on bran. If he was feeling indulgent, he would soak the bran in some port wine. At the end of the week the snails would be purged of any unpleasant material they might have consumed. Peter would collect up the unsuspecting creatures and take them to Mrs Cadogan. She would set about preparing them.

―――――――――――――INGREDIENTS―――――――――――――

snails (recommended 6 per person)   salt and pepper
thyme, rosemary, savoury, parsley   butter

―――――――――――――METHOD―――――――――――――

Drop the snails into a pot of boiling water, to kill them painlessly. After 2 minutes remove the snails from the water and take them from their shells. Reserve and clean the shells. Wash the snails in about 12 changes of water or until the water turns clear. Then, put them into a pot of water with sprigs of thyme, rosemary, savoury and parsley, salt and pepper. Bring to the boil and simmer for 1 hour. When the hour is up, change the water and repeat the process with fresh herbs for a further hour. Then drain the snails and put them back into their shells. Meanwhile, heat up some butter with more herbs, chopped this time, salt and pepper. Pour this herb butter into the shells, over the hot snails, and serve.

Shreelane Soufflés

―――――――――――――INGREDIENTS―――――――――――――

3 eggs, separated   ½ tablespoon powdered gelatine
½ pint (300 ml) milk   3 tablespoons double cream
pinch of cayenne pepper   8 oz (225 g) fresh prawns
anchovy essence

─────────────METHOD─────────────
Make a custard from the egg yolks and the milk, following the method on page 88; flavour with cayenne pepper and anchovy essence. Put the gelatine into a bowl containing 2 tablespoons of cold water. Place this bowl into a saucepan of warm water and heat gently until the gelatine dissolves. Pour the custard into a bowl and stir in the gelatine, add the cream and set aside until the mixture begins to set. Add the prawns, beat the egg whites stiffly and fold in. Put this mixture into 4 small ramekins and leave to set in the refrigerator. Serve with warm toast and butter. *Serves 4.*

Eggs Phouka

─────────────INGREDIENTS─────────────
6 duck eggs
¼ pint (150 ml) double cream
finely chopped herbs: e.g. parsley,
   chervil, tarragon

celery salt
salt
juice of ½ lemon

─────────────METHOD─────────────
Hard-boil the eggs then split them in half lengthwise. Remove the yolks and sieve them. Mash the egg yolks with the cream and chopped herbs of your choice. Season to taste with celery salt, salt and the lemon juice. Fill the cavities of the eggs with the mixture. *Serves 6.*

Basil Leigh Kelway's Stuffed Mussels

'Basil Leigh Kelway was collecting statistics for his chief on various points connected with the liquor question in Ireland ... I did my best for Leigh Kelway. I turned him loose on Father Scanlan; I showed him Mohona, our champion village, that boasts fifteen public houses out of twenty buildings of sorts and a railway station; I took him to hear the prosecution of a publican for selling drink on a Sunday, which gave him the opportunity of studying perjury as a fine art, and of hearing a lady, on whom police suspicion justly rested, profoundly summed up by the sergeant as "a woman who had th'appairance of having knocked at a back door".'

Some Experiences of an Irish R.M.

---INGREDIENTS---

1 quart mussels   1 clove garlic
2 oz (50 g) butter   a little coarse salt
1 oz (25 g) fresh breadcrumbs   1 tablespoon chopped parsley

---METHOD---

Thoroughly clean then open the mussels by shaking them in a pan over a moderate heat. Remove half the shell from each. Melt the butter in a pan and turn the breadcrumbs in it till they absorb it all. Crush the clove of garlic to a paste with the salt. Add it and the parsley to the breadcrumbs, loosely fill the shells with this mixture and brown under the grill. *Serves 4.*

Aussolas Salad

---INGREDIENTS---

4 pints (2 litres) mussels   1½ tablespoons wine vinegar
a handful of parsley   3 tablespoons oil
2 shallots or 1 small onion   salt and pepper

---METHOD---

Wash and scrub the mussels, discarding those which do not open. Chop half the parsley; peel and chop the shallots or onion. Put the mussels into a large pan with the unchopped parsley. Without adding any liquid, cook the mussels for 2 or 3 minutes over a high heat, just until they open. Then drain them, reserving the cooking juices.

Remove the mussels from their shells and arrange them in 4 individual bowls. For the dressing, mix together in a bowl the chopped shallots or onion and parsley, the mussel cooking juices, the oil and vinegar, a little salt and plenty of pepper. Sprinkle this sauce over the mussels and serve. *Serves 4.*

Salmony Cases

INGREDIENTS
---

4 oz (100 g) smoked salmon
2 oz (50 g) butter
¼ onion, finely chopped
juice of ½ lemon

1 tablespoon chopped parsley
12 small tomatoes
salt and pepper

METHOD

Finely chop the smoked salmon and mix it with the softened butter, onion, lemon juice and parsley. Blanch the tomatoes briefly in boiling water, skin them and slice off their tops. Remove the pulp, season, and fill the cases with the salmon mixture. Put the tops back onto the tomatoes and bake them in a hot oven, 400°F (200°C, gas mark 6) for about 5 minutes. *Serves 4 to 6.*

MEAT DISHES

Mrs Cadogan's Irish Stew

This recipe has been in Mrs Cadogan's family for generations. Her ancestors lived in small cabins with only a frying pan, griddle and potato-pot for cooking. It was not often that they had meat at their table and so the meal would have been quite an occasion.

INGREDIENTS

2 lb (1 kg) neck of mutton
1 lb (450 g) potatoes
6 onions

salt and pepper
parsley

METHOD

Chop up the meat, wash and peel the potatoes and peel the onions. Put the meat, 1 sliced potato and 1 sliced onion into a saucepan. Season to taste and pour on ¾ pint (350 ml) water. Simmer for 1 hour. Then put in the rest of the potatoes and onions and simmer for a further hour. When serving put the meat in the centre of the dish and surround it with the potatoes and onions. Garnish with parsley. *Serves 4.*

Castletownshend Neck of Lamb

INGREDIENTS

2 oz (50 g) butter
3 lb (1 kg 450 g) best end neck of
   lamb
2 glasses red wine
1 onion, chopped

1 clove garlic
½ oz (15 g) plain flour
½ pint (300 ml) stock
1 tablespoon tomato purée
1 teaspoon chopped fresh herbs

─────────────────METHOD─────────────────

Grease a roasting tin with 1 oz (25 g) of the butter. Remove the bones from the meat, put it into the greased tin, and add a glass of red wine. Cook for 1 hour, 400°F (200°C, gas mark 6), and baste well.

To make the sauce, melt the remaining butter and gently fry the onion, add the garlic. Add the flour and stir over a gentle heat until golden brown. Add the stock and gradually pour in a glass of red wine. Bring to the boil and add the tomato purée. Simmer for 5 minutes. Put through a sieve, add the herbs and serve poured over the meat. *Serves 4–6.*

Roaring Jack's Roast Lamb

'Mr Mooney, solicitor for the Brickleys, widely known and respected as "Roaring Jack", was in possession of that much-enduring organ, the ear of the court.'

Experiences of an Irish R.M.

─────────────────INGREDIENTS─────────────────

4 lb (2 kg) gigot of lamb (with breast)	3 oz (75 g) chopped onion
fresh rosemary leaves	8 oz (225 g) long-grain rice
2 cloves garlic, chopped	4 oz (100 g) dried chopped apricots
salt and black pepper	2 tablespoons raisins
Stuffing	½ teaspoon cinnamon
1 oz (25 g) butter	salt and pepper

─────────────────METHOD─────────────────

Bone the lamb and strew it liberally with rosemary and chopped garlic. Season with salt and freshly ground black pepper.

To make the stuffing: melt the butter and cook the onion in it until softened, 5 minutes or so. Stir in the rice and add 1 pint (600 ml) water. Bring to a boil, then simmer gently until tender. Mix with the rest of the stuffing ingredients. Stuff the lamb with this mixture and roll it up, beginning at the gigot end. Secure well, with skewers or string, and roast as for an ordinary joint, allowing 20 minutes per pound (half kilo), stuffed weight, plus 20 minutes over at 400°F (200°C, gas mark 6) . When it is done, remove the roast to a serving dish. Pour the fat from the pan juices, mix in any rice mixture that may have been left over, and reheat. Serve with, or around, the lamb. *Serves 6.*

Lamb with Claret

'She declined to correct the phraseology of the parlourmaid, whose painful habit it was to whisper "Do ye choose cherry or clarry?" when proferring the wine.'

Some Experiences of an Irish R.M.

────────────────────INGREDIENTS────────────────────

2½ lb (1·25 kg) shoulder of lamb   1 lb (450 g) button mushrooms
8 oz (225 g) piece of streaky bacon   2 oz (50 g) butter
1 bottle of claret   salt and pepper
1 lb (450 g) small firm onions

──────────────────────METHOD──────────────────────

Cut the lamb into large cubes. Put it into a casserole with the bacon, cut into strips, and brown them lightly on all sides. Pour over the wine and add the bouquet garni and a little salt. Cover, bring to a boil on the stove, then put into a moderate oven 325°F (160°C, gas mark 3) for 1 hour. Regulate the oven temperature so that the dish simmers gently.

Meanwhile gently sauté the mushrooms and onions in the butter until golden. Add to the lamb and continue to cook for a further hour. *Serves 4.*

Spiced Beef O'Rourke

At Christmas parties in Ireland, spiced beef is served. Mrs Cadogan indulges in Christmas revelry with some reluctance. She only really approves of the highest spirits at wakes and funerals. If those around her get too excited she will tell the cautionary tale of O'Rourke's Feast.

O'Rourke's noble feast
Can ne'er be forgot
By those who were there
Or those who were not.

His revels to keep
We sip and we dine
On seven score sheep
Fat bullocks, and swine.

Poteen to our feast
In pails was brought up
A hundred at least
And a vessel our cup.

Come harper strike up!
But first by your favour,
Boy, give us a cup,
Ah! this has some savour.

Good lord, what a sight!
After all this good cheer
For people to fight
In the midst of their beer.

They rise from their feast,
And hot are their brains,
A cubit at least
The length of their skeans.*

What stabs and what cuts,
What clattering of sticks,
What cracking of ribs,
What bastings and kicks.

With cudgels of oak,
Well hardened in flame,
A hundred heads broke
A hundred legs lame.

Ask this woman here
She'll tell you who's who
As far up as Adam
She knows it is true!

*skeans = long knives

INGREDIENTS

7 lb (3·5 kg) boned round steak
6 shallots
4 dried bay leaves
1 teaspoon powdered cloves
1 teaspoon powdered mace
½ teaspoon peppercorns

1 teaspoon allspice
½ teaspoon thyme
3 tablespoons brown sugar
1 lb (450 g) coarse salt
2 teaspoons potassium nitrate
2 tablespoons treacle

METHOD

Chop the shallots and bay leaves very finely and add in all the ingredients except for the meat and treacle. Rub the mixture into the meat and leave to marinate for 2 days, turning regularly. Pour the treacle over the meat at this stage and proceed to rub the mixture well into the meat every day for a week. When the week is up, the meat should be tied up in muslin, covered with water and gently simmered for 6 hours. Eat hot or cold. Serve with horseradish sauce (page 111). *Serves 18–20.*

Beef Knox

---INGREDIENTS---

1 lb (450 g) lean beef
1 oz (25 g) flour
salt and pepper
1 oz (25 g) butter
4 oz (100 g) onion, sliced

½ pint (300 ml) beer
1 pint (600 ml) beef stock
½ oz (15 g) caster sugar
¼ pint (150 ml) double cream

---METHOD---

Chop the meat into 1-inch (2-cm) cubes. Season the flour and toss the meat in it. Melt the butter in a pan and fry the meat in it. Place the meat in a casserole dish. Fry the onion in the same butter until light brown then add to the meat. Gently boil together the beer and stock and add the caster sugar, stirring all the time. Pour this mixture over the beef and onions and cover. Cook in a moderate oven 350°F (180°C, gas mark 4) for 3 hours. Just before serving whip up the cream and float dollops of it on the beef. *Serves 3–4.*

Slipper's Whiskey Steak

Slipper enjoyed his drink, and would have highly approved of this recipe as uniting the good things of life.

'"Major Yeates!" he began, "and Mrs Major Yeates, with respex to ye, I'm bastely dhrunk! Me head is light since the 'fluenzy, and the doctor told me I should carry a little bottleen o' sperrits –"

'Slipper was getting drunker every moment, but I managed to stow him on his back in the bows of the punt, in which position he at once began to uplift husky and wandering strains of melody. To this accompaniment we, as Tennyson says,

> moved from the brink, like some full-breasted swan,
> That, fluting a wild carol ere her death,
> Ruffles her pure cold plume, and takes the flood
> With swarthy web.

'Slipper would certainly have been none the worse for taking the flood, and, as the burden of *Lannigan's Ball* spread and strengthened along the tranquil lake, and the duck once more fled in justifiable consternation, I felt much inclined to make him do so.'

Some Experiences of an Irish R.M.

────────────────INGREDIENTS────────────────

Per person

2 teaspoons black peppercorns, crushed
1 piece fillet steak, about 8 oz (225 g)

coil
3 tablespoons Irish whiskey
2 tablespoons single cream
chopped parsley

────────────────METHOD────────────────

Rub the crushed black peppercorns into the steak. Heat up the oil until it gives wisps of smoke, and fry the steak for 3 minutes on each side. Drain off all the fat, pour on the whiskey and light it, cooking for a final minute. Remove the steak from the pan and keep it hot; quickly pour the cream into the pan, add the parsley and mix well together. Serve the steak and pour the sauce over it.

Curranhilty Veal Escalopes

────────────────INGREDIENTS────────────────

6 veal escalopes
salt and pepper
2 tablespoons oil

2 tablespoons sherry
1 tablespoon mild French mustard
3 tablespoons double cream

────────────────METHOD────────────────

Season the escalopes with salt and pepper and sauté them in the oil until they are golden and half-cooked. Then add the sherry and continue to sauté until almost done. Then mix together the mustard and cream and pour around and under the meat. Cook for a few minutes to reduce and thicken the sauce a little. Check the seasoning and adjust if necessary, then serve very hot, right away, with lightly cooked green vegetables or rice. *Serves 6.*

Dublin Coddle

────────────────INGREDIENTS────────────────

1 oz (25 g) fat
4 oz (100 g) bacon, chopped
12 oz (350 g) onions

1 lb (450 g) small potatoes
1 pint (600 ml) stock
salt and pepper

—————————————————————METHOD—————————————————————

Melt the fat and fry the chopped bacon and onions together in it; cook until the onions are golden brown. Meanwhile peel the potatoes and add to the onions and bacon along with the stock. Season, cover and simmer until the potatoes are tender. *Serves 2–3.*

Gammon Steak Knox

Flurry Knox likes to tell a story about one of his ancestors, who was visiting England. The Mr Knox of the day ordered his dinner in a country pub within hearing of two lively-looking Englishmen.

The waiter delivered two large covered dishes, containing potatoes. It was not what Mr Knox had ordered. He asked the waiter why so many potatoes, and no other food, had been put before him. The waiter indicated towards the two men at the bar. Mr Knox nodded, and ate his way steadily through the mounds of potatoes.

Just as Mr Knox was finishing his meal, the two grinning Englishmen themselves became the recipients of two large covered dishes. They raised the covers and found two pistols. Flurry's relative thanked them for their hospitality, and begged permission to exchange shots with them, one at a time. The humorous gentlemen quickly fled the premises, and Flurry's ancestor ordered more potatoes, along with a leg of lamb and some gammon steak.

—————————————————————INGREDIENTS—————————————————————

4 gammon steaks	½ pint (300 ml) soured cream
4 oz (100 g) butter	paprika
2 cooking apples	salt and pepper

—————————————————————METHOD—————————————————————

Grill the steaks for 8 minutes on each side. Melt the butter, cut the apples into rings and fry the apple rings for 3 minutes a side. Arrange 2 apple rings on each steak and spoon the soured cream over. Season with paprika, salt and pepper. *Serves 4.*

Slipper's Savoury Pork

This simple and traditional recipe might go some way towards contradicting the words of one great Irishman, George Bernard Shaw. He said, 'I do not eat cooked food. I have not tasted fish, flesh or fowl for 60 years past. All the cookery books known to me, including the vegetarian ones, describe so many ingredients that they could be of use only to a universal grocer, butcher or international provision business'.

---INGREDIENTS---

½ lb (225 g) onions, thinly sliced
½ lb (225 g) carrots, thinly sliced
1 oz (25g) dripping
4 pork steaks

salt and pepper
1 teaspoon sage
4 apples, peeled, cored and sliced

---METHOD---

Place the prepared vegetables in a casserole with the dripping. Season the pork steaks and place them in it also, with the sage and apple slices. Add enough water to cover the base of the casserole by ½ inch (1·25 cm), cover and cook in a preheated hot oven, 425°F (220°C, gas mark 7) until the liquid comes to the boil. Then lower the heat to moderate, 325°F (160°C, gas mark 3) and simmer gently for a further ½ hour. *Serves 4.*

Baked Ham with Apples à la Christopher

Just before Christmas one year, Lady Knox grudgingly gave her permission to her butler to go back to his home village to visit his ailing mother. As this meant the absence of a key domestic servant over a period in which entertainment of guests is almost obligatory in Ireland, Lady Knox moved quickly to obtain the temporary services of another butler. A substitute was produced, by name of Christopher. It would be an exaggeration to say Christopher was an experienced butler, but he had once helped to carry drinks around at a Hunt Ball.

All went well, until New Year's Eve. Some of the more desirable Knox relatives were to come to dinner, and Lady Knox decided that a roast sucking pig should be prepared. Christopher tactfully asked how he should serve the sucking pig. His Mistress replied, 'As a rule rather dressed up, you know, an apple in the mouth and parsley behind the ears.'

The large party of Knoxes were seated around the Castle Knox dining table, eagerly awaiting the splendid feast. The double doors of the dining room swung open, revealing Christopher bearing an ungarnished sucking pig on a shining silver platter. The replacement butler had an apple in his mouth and half the contents of the herb garden behind his ear.

---------------------------------INGREDIENTS---------------------------------

1 Limerick ham weighing about 6–   parsley
  7 lb (3 kg)   thyme
½ pint (300 ml) vinegar   12 cloves
4 pints (2·3 litres) cider   1 clove garlic
3 onions, chopped   2 oz (50 g) brown sugar
bay leaf

---------------------------------METHOD---------------------------------

Steep the ham in cold water for 24 hours. Drain it. Boil up the vinegar and cider with the onions, bay leaf, parsley, thyme, garlic and 1 oz (25 g) of sugar. Pour this mixture over the ham and bake in a moderate oven, 350°F (180°C, gas mark 4), allowing 30 minutes for each pound (500 g) of ham, with 30 minutes extra at the end. When the ham is cooked, take it from the oven and remove the rind. Stick in the cloves and sprinkle with the remaining brown sugar. Put the ham back into the hot oven until brown. Meanwhile, reduce the liquid to a glaze and pour this over the ham before serving. This can be served with baked apples, which should be arranged around the ham. *Serves 18–20.*

Peter Cadogan's Pig

The pig is Peter Cadogan's favourite animal. Peter finds it difficult to concentrate on anything. Indeed, seldom can he think what it is he should be doing. Most of Peter's time is spent trying to remember what he has forgotten. In the pig, he recognizes a great dedication and mastery of one subject – food. The pig lives to eat. He eats only to die. He eats everything his nose touches, and he in turn will one day be eaten completely. He eats all the time, all the time he will be eaten.

The pig is an immense dish which eats while waiting to be eaten. Peter Cadogan admires the pig.

---INGREDIENTS---

3 pork steaks weighing about 7 oz (200 g) each
2 oz (50 g) walnuts
4 oz (100 g) fresh breadcrumbs

2 teaspoons dried thyme
18 oz (500 g) mandarins
2 tablespoons oil

---METHOD---

Cut the pork steaks in half and beat them to flatten them. Chop the walnuts and mix them with the breadcrumbs and thyme. Squeeze out the mandarin juice and use sufficient of it to bind the mixture. Spread the mixture on the pork steaks, roll them up and secure with skewers. Roast in oil and the remaining mandarin juice in a 400°F (200°C, gas mark 6) oven for 1 hour, basting frequently. *Serves 3.*

Pork Ciste Cadogan

Mrs Cadogan's family kept pigs which, in the Irish custom, were left to wander freely in and out of the cabin. One day they ate the beer grounds out of an old barrel. They became extremely drunk. They were not able to stand and soon lost consciousness. The next day they were a little better, but still stumbled all over the yard. They took four days to recover fully. It was generally agreed that nobody had ever seen pigs so drunk.

---INGREDIENTS---

8 pork chops
4 pork kidneys
2 carrots
3 onions
1 tablespoon chopped parsley
1 tablespoon chopped thyme
1 bay leaf

salt and pepper
1 pint (600 ml) stock
8 oz (225 g) flour
4 oz (100 g) grated suet
1 teaspoon baking powder
½ teaspoon salt
about 4 fl oz (100 ml) milk

──────────────────────────METHOD──────────────────────────

Remove the fat from the chops and arrange them in the base of a casserole, around the edge. Chop the kidneys, slice the carrots and onions, and put them in the centre of the pan along with the herbs. Season, cover with stock and simmer for 30 minutes.

Meanwhile, prepare the ciste* by first making a stiffish dough by mixing the flour, suet, baking powder and salt together with the milk. Roll the ciste out to the size and shape of the casserole. Put the ciste on top of the meat and vegetables and press it tightly down. Cover and cook gently for 1½ hours. *Serves 4–6.*

Mrs Cadogan's Cassoulet

Major Yeates in the course of his travels in France had acquired a great fondness for cassoulet and, upon setting up his own establishment with his own cook, determined to enjoy it often at his table. Mrs Cadogan was a willing pupil and did her best to recreate the dish as perfectly as she knew. The spicy sausages of the original were beyond her, but soon the Major became so used to her substitute, pig's trotters, that it was not long before he thought it superior to the French version.

──────────────────────────INGREDIENTS──────────────────────────

1 lb (450 g) haricot beans	salt and pepper
4 pig's trotters	2–3 tablespoons dripping or butter
1 whole onion, peeled	1 chopped onion
3–4 cloves	1 lb (450 g) tomatoes
4 cloves garlic	1 lb (450 g) pork sausages
bouquet garni	

──────────────────────────METHOD──────────────────────────

Soak the beans overnight in salted water.

Place the pig's trotters in a large pan of water, bring to a boil and drain. Rinse the pan, replace the trotters, add the whole onion (stuck with the cloves), garlic, bouquet garni, and salt and pepper. Cover well with water, bring to the boil and simmer for 2 hours or until the meat is very tender. Strain, reserving the stock.

In a large saucepan heat the dripping and cook the chopped onion in it until soft. Split the trotters and add them also, with the tomatoes, skinned and quartered, and the drained beans. Moisten with some of the stock and simmer very slowly for 3 hours, adding more stock from time to time to keep it from getting dry. Taste for seasoning.

─────────────────

* 'cake'

Transfer the cassoulet to a large casserole. Halve the pork sausages, fry them until brown and arrange them over the top. Cook in a moderate oven, 350°F (180°C, gas mark 4) for about 1 hour. When it is ready the liquid will be almost all absorbed except for some around the edges. *Serves 8.*

Leanhaun Shee Sweetbread Pie

────────────────INGREDIENTS────────────────

1 teaspoon vinegar
1 lb (450 g) sweetbreads
shortcrust pastry made with 4 oz
    (100 g) flour, 2 oz (50 g) butter
    and a little water
2 oz (50 g) butter

4 oz (100 g) button mushrooms,
    halved
1½ tablespoons capers
1 oz (25 g) breadcrumbs, crisply fried
    in butter

────────────────METHOD────────────────

Soak the sweetbreads in frequently changed cold water for at least 1 hour. Then trim off any membrane and 'tubes'.

Acidulate some water by adding vinegar to it and gently simmer the sweetbreads in it until tender, about 15 minutes.

Make a shortcrust pastry dough by rubbing the butter into the flour until it resembles breadcrumbs, then mix to a dough with a tablespoon or two of cold water. Roll out and line a shallow, small pie dish and bake in a moderate oven, 375°F (190°C, gas mark 5) for 10 minutes or so.

Melt the butter and gently fry the sweetbreads, mushrooms and capers in it for 8 minutes. Then turn into the pie dish and top with the fried breadcrumbs. Serve immediately. *Serves 2.*

POULTRY AND GAME

Philippa's Healthy Chicken

One of the books that Philippa Yeates brought with her to Ireland was the *Sunlight Year Book*. This book, to Mrs Cadogan's disgust, gave all sorts of useful English domestic advice. Very little of this was practical in Ireland!

Philippa did, however, attempt to heed its advice on beauty care, which ran as follows:

'The fatal gift of beauty is vouchsafed to only a few, for it is rarely one meets a really beautiful face. But to those who are anxious to make the best of themselves, a few hints may be useful.

1. All highly seasoned, rich dishes should be avoided, as should also beer and spirits.
2. Rainwater, when possible, should be used to wash in.
3. Tight lacing is simply ruinous to the complexion, and a red nose will often result if it is persisted in.'

This chicken dish is not highly seasoned or rich, and the *Sunlight Year Book* did not mention cider!

---INGREDIENTS---

2 tablespoons butter	salt and pepper
2 tablespoons flour	4 bay leaves
15 fl oz (400 ml) dry cider	½ teaspoon ground nutmeg
1 chicken, weighing about 3¾ lb	2 peeled shallots
(1·8 kg)	8 oz (225 g) button mushrooms

METHOD

Take a casserole and melt the butter in it. Stir in the flour. Add in enough still cider to make a smooth sauce that would come half way up the chicken. Lay the chicken on its side in the casserole, half-covered by the sauce. Add salt and pepper, the bay leaves and nutmeg to the sauce. Cover the pot and put it in a moderate oven, 350°F (180°C, gas mark 4) for 2 hours (or until tender). After 30 minutes add the shallots and the mushrooms, previously chopped and softened in butter over a low heat. *Serves 5–6.*

Mrs Dunne's Chicken

When Mrs Cadogan started out in service, she worked as a kitchen maid under a Mrs Dunne in a house near Skibbereen, County Cork. Mrs Dunne was a great cook as this recipe bears witness, but she did like a drop or two of the porter every evening while she was preparing dinner. She would keep the bottle under the kitchen table, and take swigs from it as she worked.

One afternoon the young Mrs Cadogan was scrubbing the floor of the kitchen with Jeyes Fluid, when she was called away to help with preparations for tea. She left the bottle of Jeyes Fluid under the kitchen table.

That evening Mrs Dunne reached under the table, between basting the chicken and making the gravy, and took a swig from the bottle. The results were spectacular. Jeyes Fluid spewed everywhere, the bottle crashed to the floor and Mrs Dunne let out a wail. She was a devout and simple Catholic and she realized she was being punished for her intemperence. So she went to her room and prepared to surrender herself to her maker.

Some time later, the Lady of the house came down to the kitchen to see how preparations for dinner were progressing. Finding the kitchen empty and unprepared, she went to find the cook. She found Mrs Dunne in her room. She had changed into a brown robe, the sort worn by corpses at funerals. She was lying face upwards on her bed, her hands clasped around a lighted candle on her chest, her eyes open, waiting for the Lord, in his wisdom, to take her away!

──────────────────────INGREDIENTS──────────────────────

8 oz (200 g) veal   2 tablespoons brandy
4 oz (100 g) ham   1 egg
4 oz (100 g) chicken liver   2 oz (50 g) butter
1 onion   4-lb (2-kg) chicken
4–6 tablespoons lemon juice   salt and pepper
1 tablespoon chopped parsley

──────────────────────METHOD──────────────────────

Mince together the veal, ham and chicken liver. Peel the onion, chop it up and add to the minced ingredients to make a stuffing mixture. Add the lemon juice, parsley and brandy. Lightly beat the egg and use it to bind the stuffing.

Fill the chicken with stuffing, and truss or sew it together with thread. Grease a roasting tin and place the chicken in it seam-side down. Melt the butter and brush it over the chicken. Season. Cover with foil and bake at 400°F (200°C, gas mark 6) for 1½ hours. Remove the foil after 1 hour to brown. *Serves 4–5.*

Chicken Luggala

──────────────────────INGREDIENTS──────────────────────

3-lb (1·5-kg) chicken   2 leeks, chopped
flour   4 oz (100 g) mushrooms
salt and pepper   ½ pint (300 ml) cider
2 oz (50 g) butter   ½ pint (300 ml) double cream
2 slices bacon   watercress

──────────────────────METHOD──────────────────────

Skin the raw chicken and cut it into portions. Dip these portions in seasoned flour. Melt the butter and cook the chicken pieces in it until they are a light brown colour, remove from the pan. Dice the bacon and fry likewise. Add the leeks and mushrooms. When they are cooked, add the cider and the cream. Reduce the sauce and return the chicken to it, simmering for a few minutes. Serve garnished with watercress. *Serves 4.*

The R.M.'s Turkey Escalopes

―――――――――――――――INGREDIENTS―――――――――――――――

8 oz (225 g) button mushrooms	3 tablespoons port
1½ oz (40 g) butter	salt and pepper
4 turkey escalopes, weighing about	½ teaspoon mustard
5 oz (150 g) each	2 tablespoons double cream

―――――――――――――――METHOD―――――――――――――――

Wash the mushrooms, dry and slice them finely. Melt the butter in a large frying pan, put in the escalopes and brown them for 3 or 4 minutes on each side over a fairly high heat. Add the mushrooms to the pan, around the escalopes, and cook them over a high heat until their juices run. Pour over the port, season with salt and pepper and continue to cook for 5 minutes or so more.

Remove the turkey escalopes and keep them warm on a serving dish; mix the mustard with the cream and stir into the pan in their place. Allow to thicken for 2 or 3 minutes over a moderately high heat. Pour this sauce over the escalopes and serve right away, with plain boiled or steamed potatoes. *Serves 4.*

Duck Ned Flaherty

'"Sing up, Paddy Boy, for the gentleman! Arrah, what ails ye Paddy! Don't be ashamed at all!"

'"Tis a lovely song, your honour, sir!" (this to my brother-in-law).

'"Is it an ancient song?"

'"It is your honour; 'twas himself made it up lasht year, and he sings it beautiful! Oh! Paddy's a perfect modulator!"

'... The modulator opened with a long-draen and nasal cadenza, suggestive of the droning preliminary canter of a bagpipe, which merged into the statement that

> The poor little fella',
> His legs they were yella',
> His bosom was blue, he could swim like a hake;
> But some wicked savage,
> To grease his white cabbage,
> Murdered Ned Flaherty's beautiful dhrake!'

Further Experiences of an Irish R.M.

────────────────────INGREDIENTS────────────────────

2 ducks, weighing 3–3½ lb (1·5–
　1·75 kg) each
3 oz (75 g) butter
2 onions
2 carrots
bouquet garni
2 tablespoons Irish whiskey

½ pint (300 ml) chicken stock
½ pint (300 ml) brown sauce (page
　110)
½ pint (300 ml) tomato sauce (page
　111)
8 oz (225 g) mushrooms
salt and pepper

────────────────────METHOD────────────────────

Joint the duck and roast until half cooked. To cook completely, allow
15 minutes per pound (500 g) in a moderate oven 375°F (190°C, gas
mark 5). Melt 2 oz of the butter and pour it into an ovenproof dish.
Slice the onions and carrots and add them to the butter along with the
bouquet garni. Lay the duck pieces on top and cook in the oven at
350°F (180°C, gas mark 4) for another 20 minutes. Strain off the
buttery cooking juices, add the whiskey, stock and sauces. Melt the
remaining butter and sauté the mushrooms in it. Cover the duck with
the mushrooms, season and serve. *Serves 6–8.*

The Dispensary Doctor's Wild Duck

A simple dish in honour of a fine man:

'In Memoriam – Alex Slorach Belakley, A.B., M.B., T.C.D., J.P.,
For 23 years Medical Officer of Blessington and Ballymore-Eustace
Dispensary Districts, who died 28th April, 1901, and was here
interred. Able in his profession, unselfish, benevolent, and daily
practising an extensive charity towards the suffering poor, he was
greatly esteemed. His numerous friends have erected this Memorial to
a noble life.'

On a gravestone in Blessington churchyard

────────────────────INGREDIENTS────────────────────

1 wild duck
2 tablespoons softened butter
1 glass red wine

1 orange, squeezed out
salt and pepper
½ wine glass brandy

————————————METHOD————————————

Smear the bird with butter and roast in a moderate oven, 375°F (190°C, gas mark 5), for 15 minutes. Add the red wine, the juice of the orange, salt and pepper. Roast for a further 15 minutes. Reduce the gravy down, while keeping the bird warm. Mix in ½ a wine glass of brandy just before serving. *Serves 2.*

Christmas Goose

Mrs Cadogan's family always had goose for lunch on Christmas Day. She knew that the goose was good eating at that time of year.

> Geese now in their prime season are,
> Which if well roasted are good fare;
> Yet, however, friends take heed,
> How too much on them you feed,
> Lest when as your tongues run loose
> Your discourse do smell of goose.

Preparation for Christmas lunch would start some two weeks in advance. One of the Cadogan geese was locked in an empty shed overnight. In the morning, with an empty crop, the goose was killed. It would be plucked and singed, hung up by its feet for a week. The bird would then be drawn and its head removed. It would then be prepared for roasting.

————————————INGREDIENTS————————————

1 goose weighing about 10 lb (4·5 kg)	dripping
potato stuffing (see page 58)	1 tablespoon flour
salt and pepper	¾ pint (450 ml) hot stock

————————————METHOD————————————

Fill the bird with potato stuffing (see page 58). Then season and truss it, using skewers. Put one through the end of a wing, pressing through the body and out, skewering the other wing. The other skewer is passed through the first joint of the legs in the same way. Turn the skin of the neck down over the back and secure with trussing string or thread. Heat up dripping in a roasting tin until it is smoking hot. Baste the goose with this, and place it breast down in the tin. Place in a preheated moderate oven, 375°F (190°C, gas mark 5), for about 2½ hours, covering with foil if getting too brown, basting frequently. Turn breast up after 1½ hours. Just before removing from oven to serve, turn the heat right up to brown the skin.

Finally, make a gravy by pouring off the fat from the roasting tin, stirring in the flour and cooking for a few minutes over a moderate heat. Add the stock gradually and simmer the gravy for 5 minutes or so, stirring well. Serve separately. *Serves 6.*

Potato stuffing for the goose

1 lb (450 g) mashed potato	salt and pepper
3 medium onions, chopped	1 tablespoon chopped fresh sage
2 oz (50 g) butter	

Make the stuffing by first of all preparing the mashed potato. Then sauté the onion in the butter until soft, and mix well into the potato, adding the salt, pepper and sage. Stuff the goose with this mixture and secure or cover the opening before cooking.

Skebawn Roast Pheasant

When the young pheasant, felled by the Major's gun, was brought into the kitchen at Skebawn, the tail feathers would be removed and made into a 'Turk's head'.

The feathers would be attached firmly with string to the end of a very long pole, and used for cleaning cornices, high ceilings and stubborn cobwebs.

──────────────── INGREDIENTS ────────────────

1 young pheasant	flour
salt and pepper	4–6 slices of fatty bacon
1 oz (25 g) butter	

──────────────── METHOD ────────────────

Draw the pheasant and truss it if this has not already been done for you. Season with salt and pepper inside and out. Melt the butter. Cover the breast with flour and brown it in the butter. Tie the thin, fatty rashers of bacon to the breast. Wrap in foil and roast in a medium oven, 350°F (180°C, gas mark 4), for about 45 minutes. Remove from the oven and baste well, before returning it to a hot oven, 400°F (200°C, gas mark 6), for a further 15 minutes. Serve with cranberry sauce (page 112). *Serves 2–3.*

If the bird is basted sufficiently and is not overcooked there is no finer way to cook a pheasant.

Grilled Plover

'At length, through the crannies of a wall, I perceived just within shot a stand of plover, hopping, gobbling, squealing, quite unaware of my proximity. I cautiously laid my gun on the top of the wall. As I cocked it, a white form appeared on a fence behind the birds, poised itself for an instant with elf-like ears spread wide, then, volleying barks, the intolerable Minx burst like a firework into the heart of the plover. In lightning response to her comrade's tally-ho Maria rocketed over the wall; the plover rose as one man, and, as I missed with both barrels, swirled out of range and sight. By way, I suppose, of rounding off the jest effectively, Maria rushed in scientific zigzags through the field, in search of the bird that she well knew I had not shot, deaf as the dead to words of command, while Minx, stark mad with excitement, circled and shrieked round Maria. To thrash Minx was not only absurd but impossible; one might as well have tried to thrash a grasshopper.'

Further Experiences of an Irish R.M.

———————————————INGREDIENTS———————————————

1 plover per person   butter

—————————————————METHOD—————————————————

The best way to cook a plover, should you come across one, is the simplest. It requires only the bird itself and some butter. Pluck the bird, without drawing it, and smear the body with butter. Then grill it on a spit over a turf or fire for about 10 minutes each side.

Guinea Fowl with Gin

———————————————INGREDIENTS———————————————

1 oz (25 g) cream cheese	4 small bananas
4 oz (100 g) butter	2 oz (50 g) blanched almonds
salt and pepper	juice of 1 lemon
1 guinea fowl	4 fl oz (100 ml) Cork dry gin

—————————————————METHOD—————————————————

Preheat the oven to moderate, 350°F (180°C, gas mark 4). Blend the cream cheese with 1 oz (25 g) of the butter until smooth and season with a little salt and pepper. Put this into the guinea fowl and truss it.

Put the guinea fowl into a roasting tin, smear over with another 2 oz (50 g) butter and roast it for 45 minutes. Ten minutes before the end of the cooking time, peel the bananas, melt the rest of the butter in a frying pan and turn them gently in it over a moderate heat until golden. Remove and keep warm.

Remove the guinea fowl from the oven when ready. Cut into serving pieces and return to its cooking dish with the almonds. Sprinkle with the lemon juice and simmer for 5 minutes over a moderate heat. Place the guinea fowl on a serving dish with its accompanying cooking juices etc. Arrange the bananas around it. Finally, warm the gin and pour it over; set it alight and bring to the table. *Serves 4.*

The Whipper-in's Roast Venison

INGREDIENTS

2–2½ lb (1–1·25 kg)   2 cloves garlic, crushed
   haunch of venison   salt and pepper
1½ lb (700 g) new potatoes   bouquet garni
3 oz (75 g) butter   1 bunch watercress
about ½ pint (300 ml) stock

METHOD

Grate the new potatoes, plunging them as you do so into a bowl of cold water. Smear a large ovenproof dish with 2 oz (50 g) of the butter. Drain and pat dry the potato and arrange in the buttered dish. Pour over the stock and sprinkle over the garlic.

Season the venison and place on top of the potato. Put in the bouquet garni, melt the rest of the butter and pour it over. Cook in a moderate oven 350°F (180°C, gas mark 4) for 30 minutes. Raise the temperature to 400°F (200°C, gas mark 6) and brown for 10–15 minutes.

Remove the venison from the roasting dish and keep warm. Pour over the cooking juices and garnish with the watercress. *Serves 6.*

Jugged Hair

'I disclaimed the possession of any hairpins, but volunteered to go and look for some at a neighbouring cottage.

'The cottage door was shut, and my knockings were answered by a stupefied-looking elderly man. Conscious of my own absurdity, I asked him if he had any hairpins.

'"I didn't see a hare this week!", he responded in a slow bellow.

'"Hairpins!" I roared; "has your wife any hairpins?"

'"She has not". Then, as an after-thought, "She's dead these ten years."'

Some Experiences of an Irish R.M.

--------------------------------INGREDIENTS--------------------------------

1 hare	6 fl oz (175 ml) olive oil
vinegar	2 oz (50 g) butter
2 sprigs thyme	½ pint (300 ml) stock
6 cloves	bouquet garni
12 black peppercorns	2 bay leaves
1 clove garlic	6 bacon rashers
bunch of parsley	3 onions
½ bottle red wine	2 glasses port wine

----------------------------------METHOD----------------------------------

Your hare must be hung before cooking. Hang it head downwards with a bowl beneath to catch the blood. The bowl should contain a half an inch (1·25 cm) of water and a tablespoon or so of vinegar to prevent coagulation.

When you judge your hare has hung long enough, skin it and put it into a marinade: put a sprig of thyme, 4 cloves, 6 peppercorns, 1 clove of garlic and some parsley into a mixture of 2 glasses of the red wine and the olive oil. If your hare is old, it will need 48 hours to marinate, if young, no more than 12. Turn and baste it as often as possible.

When ready to cook, chop the hare into its natural joints. Dry the pieces. Melt the butter and brown the pieces. Put the hare into a large casserole with the stock, ½ pint (300 ml) of the original marinade, the blood, a glass of red wine, a bouquet garni, 2 bay leaves, 2 cloves and 6 peppercorns, and simmer. Meanwhile, chop and mix together the bacon rashers and the onions. Fry them in the fat used to brown the pieces of the hare. Add these to the casserole and cook for 2 to 3½ hours, depending on the age and size. The meat should come off the bone easily, but not fall off. Just before serving pour in the port. *Serves 6.*

Temple Braney Rabbit

---INGREDIENTS---

1 large rabbit	1 bay leaf
2 oz (50 g) flour	1 sprig of thyme
2 oz (50 g) butter	1 glass white wine
2 carrots, thinly sliced	salt and pepper
1 onion, thinly sliced	8 fl oz (250 ml) double cream
a few sprigs of parsley	1½ tablespoons mild mustard

---METHOD---

Cut the rabbit into serving pieces.

Put the flour onto a plate and roll the rabbit pieces in it. Melt the butter in a casserole and brown them on all sides. Remove and add the carrot, onion, parsley, thyme and bay leaf and cook for 5 minutes. Return the rabbit pieces to the pan, with the white wine and enough water to half-cover the rabbit. Bring to a boil, then cover and place in a moderate oven, 350°F (150°C, gas mark 3). Regulate the heat so that the casserole cooks gently for 40 minutes.

When cooked remove the rabbit to a shallow serving dish and keep warm. Add the cream to the casserole and thicken the sauce over moderate heat, stirring all the time; do not allow to boil. Finally push through a sieve. Stir in the mustard and pour this sauce over the rabbit. *Serves 4.*

Flurry's Rabbit Fricassée

1 large rabbit	8 fl oz (250 ml) stock
4 oz (100 g) butter	8 fl oz (250 ml) white wine
3 carrots, finely chopped	salt and pepper
1 onion, finely chopped	2 tablespoons tomato purée
1 stick celery, thinly sliced	8 oz (225 g) mushrooms
8 oz (225 g) piece streaky bacon	1 tablespoon chopped parsley
3 oz (75 g) flour	

——————————————METHOD——————————————

Cut the rabbit into serving pieces. Melt 2oz (50g) of the butter in a frying pan and brown the rabbit pieces in it on all sides. In another pan, melt another 2oz (50g) butter and soften in it for 5 minutes or so the carrot, onion and celery. Add the bacon, cut in strips, and cook, stirring, for a few minutes. Next, add the flour, stock, white wine and season with salt and pepper. Bring to a boil, add the tomato purée and stir it in, cover and cook over a gentle heat for 35 minutes.

Melt the rest of the butter in a small pan, cook the mushrooms over moderate heat for a few minutes, then add to the rabbit and continue cooking for another 10 minutes. When ready, turn into a serving dish, sprinkle with the parsley and serve right away. *Serves 4.*

Roast Woodcock

'That frosty evening was followed by three others like unto it, and a flight of woodcock came in. I calculated that I could do with five guns, and I dispatched invitations to shoot and dine on the following day to four of the local sportsmen, among whom was, of course, my landlord.'

Some Experiences of an Irish R.M.

——————————————INGREDIENTS——————————————

1 woodcock per person
melted butter
white bread

breadcrumbs
salt and pepper

——————————————METHOD——————————————

Pluck and truss your woodcock without drawing it. The head should be left on, and the long beak used to act as a skewer. Brush each plucked bird with warm butter, and place it on a thick piece of white bread. Roast in a hot oven, 400°F (200°C, gas mark 6), for 15 minutes, and serve with hot breadcrumbs, fried in butter, and bread sauce (page 112).

The Widow Twohig's Pigeon Pie

'The Widow Twohig instantly and at the top of her voice called heaven to witness her innocence, and the innocence of her "little boy"; still at full cry, she sketched her blameless career, and the unmerited suffering that had ever pursued her and hers... It was at about this point that I gave her five shillings. It was a thoroughly illogical act, but at the moment it seemed inevitable, and Mrs Twohig was good enough to accept it in the same spirit.'

Further Experiences of an Irish R.M.

-----------------------------------INGREDIENTS-----------------------------------

8 oz (225 g) veal	½ teaspoon ground mace
4 pigeons	salt and pepper
2 oz (50 g) bacon, rinds removed	½ pint (300 ml) stock
3 hard-boiled eggs	short crust pastry (page 51)
2 oz (50 g) butter	

-------------------------------------METHOD-------------------------------------

Cut the veal into pieces and put into the bottom of a deep pie dish. Clean the pigeons and remove their livers. Mince the bacon with the livers and mix in with hard-boiled egg yolks and butter, seasoned with mace, salt and pepper. Place a good dollop of this mixture inside each bird. Lay the bird on top of the veal, fill the dish with stock and cover with short crust pastry. Cook at 375°F (190°C, gas mark 5) for 25 minutes, then lower the heat to 325°F (170°C, gas mark 3) and cook for 50–60 minutes, covering the pastry if it becomes too brown. *Serves 6.*

FISH AND SHELLFISH

Philippa's Saucy Trout

'Philippa regarded Shreelane and its floundering, foundering *ménage* of incapables in the light of a gigantic picnic in a foreign land; she held long conversations daily with Mrs Cadogan, in order, as she informed me, to acquire the language; without any ulterior domestic intention she engaged kitchenmaids because of the beauty of their eyes, and housemaids because they had such delightfully picturesque old mothers, and she declined to correct the phraseology of the parlourmaid, whose painful habit it was to whisper "Do ye choose cherry or clarry?" when proferring the wine.' *Some Experiences of an Irish R.M.*

INGREDIENTS

4 trout
butter for greasing
juice of ½ lemon
salt and pepper
2 green peppers

5–6 tomatoes
1 tablespoon cooking oil
1 onion, sliced
1 clove garlic, crushed

METHOD

Clean the trout and place them in a greased ovenproof dish. Pour the lemon juice over it, season and cover with greaseproof paper. Cook in a medium oven, 350°F (180°C, gas mark 4), for 20 minutes. Meanwhile, you can prepare the sauce. Put the peppers in cold water, bring to the boil and rinse under cold running water. Do the same with the tomatoes. Then peel and slice them. Heat the oil and fry the onion in it until it is soft. Add the tomatoes and crushed garlic and season. Add the peppers when the mixture is very soft and cook for another 2 minutes. Sieve the sauce and spoon it over the trout to serve. *Serves 4.*

The Angler's Salmon

As I roved out one evening down by the river side
To catch some trout and salmon, where the streams do gently glide,
Down by the brook, along my way I there by chance did spy;
A comely maid both plain and gay just as she passed me by.

'I fear you are a stranger' she unto me did say
'Or did you come from Cupid's crew or what brought you this way?'
'Are you an angler sir?' she said 'by the river clear,
Or was it Cupid sent you here young virgins to ensnare?'

'Yes it was Cupid sent me here my fortune for to win
If I could only gain you then I'd be free from sin
From the first view I got of you my heart lies in a flame,
That's my command, give me your hand, and answer me fair maid'.

With heart and hand they waltzed along down to her father's place.
The parents they were satisfied when they first seen his face.
The banns were quickly published, and married they were for life,
Instead of trout or salmon, he brought home a virtuous wife.

---------------------------------INGREDIENTS---------------------------------

2 lb (1 kg) piece of salmon	salt and pepper
1 clove garlic, crushed	8 oz (225 g) tomatoes, chopped
1 small red chilli	1 tablespoon vinegar
cooking oil	4 fl oz (100 ml) olive oil
1 teaspoon sugar	1 tablespoon Worcester sauce
1 onion, chopped	3 oz (75 g) mushrooms
8 oz (225 g) potatoes, finely diced	

-----------------------------------METHOD-----------------------------------

This recipe is useful for salmon that have been in fresh water too long,
and whose flesh will have lost its flavour.

Remove the seeds from the chilli and chop it. Clean the salmon and
stuff with the garlic and chilli. In an ovenproof dish large enough for
the salmon, heat some oil and brown the sugar in it. In the same pan,
fry the onion briefly. Parboil the potatoes for 4 minutes. Add them and
cook gently for 10 minutes. Lay the salmon in the dish, sprinkle with
salt and pepper. Cover with the potato mixture and all the remaining
ingredients except for the mushrooms. Cover with buttered foil and
bake at 300–325°F (150–170°C, gas mark 2–3) for 40–45 minutes.
Slice the mushrooms and put them around the salmon, return to the
oven until the fish is tender. *Serves 6.*

Sea Trout with Horseradish
à la Miss Bobbie Bennett

'She had really very brilliant grey eyes, and her complexion was undeniable. Philippa has since explained to me that it is a mere male fallacy that any woman can look well with her hair down her back, but I have always maintained that Miss Bobbie Bennett, with the rain glistening on her dark tresses, looked uncommonly well.'

Some Experiences of an Irish R.M.

———————————————INGREDIENTS———————————————

1 sea trout weighing about 3 lb   1½–2 tablespoons freshly grated
  (1·5 kg)   horseradish
2 oz (50 g) butter   salt and pepper
1 tablespoon flour

———————————————METHOD———————————————

Do not scale or remove the head of the sea trout, but clean it thoroughly. Cover it with salted water, bring to a boil and simmer for 20 minutes. Drain the fish and keep warm on a serving dish. Put the liquor into a saucepan.

Quickly make the sauce. Melt the butter, add the flour and 12 fl oz (350 ml) of the fish liquor, and simmer the sauce until it is the consistency of a creamy soup and has reduced to about 8 fl oz (250 ml). Season with grated horseradish, salt and pepper and serve with the fish. *Serves 4–6.*

The Resident Magistrate's Lobster

———————————————INGREDIENTS———————————————

1 fresh lobster   ½ pint (300 ml) double cream
3 tablespoons butter   salt and pepper
4 tablespoons Irish whiskey

———————————————METHOD———————————————

Cut the lobster in two, lengthwise. Remove the meat from the tail, claws and head. Keep the shells. Cut the meat into chunks, melt the butter and cook the meat in it. Warm the whiskey, pour it over the lobster and set fire to it. Mix the cream with the pan juices, season and heat gently. Put this mixture back into the half shells and serve hot. *Serves 2.*

Lady Knox's Lobster

'Lady Knox was a short square lady, with weather-beaten face and eye decisive from long habit of taking her own line across country and elsewhere. She would have made a very imposing little coachman, and would have caused her stable helpers to rue the day they had the presumption to be born; it struck me that Sir Valentine sometimes did so.'

Some Experiences of an Irish R.M.

INGREDIENTS

4 lb (2 kg) live lobster	salt and pepper
1 carrot	6 oz (175 g) butter
1 onion	1 lemon
1 pint (600 ml) white wine	

METHOD

Kill the lobster in the way that gives you the least anguish. To give the lobster a decent send-off, it is probably kindest to put it in a saucepan of lukewarm water, and then heat it so that it dies at a low temperature. Slice the carrot and onion and mix in with the wine, 1 pint (600 ml) water and seasoning. Bring to the boil. Put the lobster in and steam them until they take on a reddish hue. Open the lobster and put the meat and all of the green juices into a bowl. Heat the butter in a saucepan and put the meat and juices into it, cooking until the juices turn pink. Spoon the meat back into the hot shells and put any remaining butter and bits into a hot sauceboat for serving separately. Garnish with lemon wedges. Eat immediately. *Serves 6–8.*

Rosse Oyster Stew

One of Mrs Cadogan's sisters was also a cook. She worked in the kitchens of the Earl of Rosse, whom she regarded as a good and kind man.

After her sister breathed the secrets of this Rosse family recipe to Mrs Cadogan, she told her also the story of Richard Parsons, 1st Earl of Rosse.

Richard Parsons had not been a good man. He was generous only with his wit which was closely allied to irreverence and obscenity. His life, so believed Mrs Cadogan's sister, was shortened by his evil practices. The local vicar wrote to the dying earl, referring to his wicked career and entreating him to turn to profit the short time remaining at his disposal by sincere repentance and fervent prayer for pardon.

Parsons read the letter, put it in a new envelope and sent it to his neighbour, the Earl of Kildare. The Earl of Kildare was a model of social and domestic virtue and was thus deeply shocked to receive such a letter. He showed the letter to the archbishop who was equally appalled. The archbishop immediately instituted proceedings to prosecute the unfortunate vicar and sent for him. Feeling sorry for his wayward cleric, the archbishop told him to write a letter of apology to the offended party.

'My Lord, how am I to ask pardon of a man who died four days ago?'

'Don't be ridiculous, man, I was talking to the Earl only this morning'.

And in this manner the joke perpetrated by one earl upon another was discovered.

INGREDIENTS

1 oz (25 g) butter	salt
2 sliced onions	½ teaspoon white pepper
1 clove garlic	cayenne pepper
1 pint (600 ml) milk	scant ¼ pint (150 ml) dry white wine
1 pint (600 ml) cream	1 teaspoon butter
1 bay leaf	paprika
2 oz (50 g) celery tops	chopped parsley
2 dozen oysters	

METHOD

Melt threequarters of the butter and fry the onions and garlic in it, until the onions turn golden. In a double saucepan, heat the milk and cream, add the cooked onions and garlic, a bay leaf, the celery tops and a third of the oysters, chopped. Stir well together and heat, without boiling, for 20 minutes. Strain the mixture, pouring the strained liquid back into the double boiler.

Put the remaining oysters into another saucepan with their juices. Add salt, white pepper and cayenne, and steam gently. The oysters are cooked when their edges start to curl. Pour them into the contents of the double saucepan, adding the white wine and a teaspoonful of butter. Heat up and serve sprinkled with paprika and parsley. *Serves 4.*

The Reverend A. B.'s Scallops

The Reverend A.B. lived in Skebawn in the late eighteenth century, and wrote, describing the old harbour:

'Their shellfish they got in the following manner; the men went to the rocks with a hook tied to the end of a strong rod; and with that they pulled from under the rocks as many crabs and lobster as they wanted; the lobster and crab commonly weighing from 5 to 12 pounds each: for scallops and oysters the young women waded into the sea, and by armfuls, brought to shore whatever number of scallops and oysters they thought requisite, the scallops weighing from 2 to 4 pounds each.'

--------------------------------INGREDIENTS--------------------------------

8 large scallops
½ pint (300 ml) white wine
2 oz (50 g) butter
8 oz (225 g) sliced mushrooms
1 oz (25 g) plain flour

salt and pepper
1 lb (500 g) potatoes, boiled and
    mashed
chopped parsley

----------------------------------METHOD----------------------------------

Wash and scrub the scallops and put them, in their shells, into a saucepan with the wine. Simmer for 5 minutes, strain off and keep the liquor. Melt the butter and lightly fry the mushrooms in it, add the flour and fry for another minute. Add the reserved liquor and gently bring it to the boil. Remove the scallops from their shells and cut the flesh into quarters, add to the liquor and heat for 5 minutes. Season to taste. Line the outside of the scallop shells with the creamed potatoes, and fill the shells with the scallops in sauce. Grill until browned and garnish with parsley. *Serves 4 as a first course or 2 as a main dish.*

A Banshee's Fish Surprise

The sound of the banshee is dreaded in Ireland. It foretells a death in the family, an imminent death. If you hear the banshee wail, most people say there is nothing you can do. But some wise old Irish women have successfully diverted the banshee from her deadly course, so this is my advice. If you hear a banshee, don't despair, go to your door and ask the banshee in. If she accepts, give her a glass of whiskey and sit her by the fire. Make her a casserole of local Irish fish, she may be able to give you a little more precious time. Try not to rush the cooking; the banshee will wait if she is hungry.

──────────────────────INGREDIENTS──────────────────────

2 onions
1 clove garlic
¼ pint (150 ml) white wine
8 oz (225 g) salmon
6 oz (175 g) any white fish
4 scallops

6 oz (175 g) prawns
1 pint of mussels
½ pint (300 ml) white sauce (page 110)
1 teaspoon fresh mixed herbs
black pepper

──────────────────────METHOD──────────────────────

Finely chop the onions and garlic. Put them in a saucepan with the wine and bring to the boil. Add the salmon and white fish and simmer. Add the scallops 4 minutes after that, the prawns 3 minutes later and remove from the heat after 1 more minute. Heat up the mussels in boiling water, making sure their shells open. Remove the fish from the pan and keep warm. Meanwhile, stir ¼ pint (150 ml) of the cooking liquid into the white sauce. Pour the sauce over the fish. Decorate with mussels and sprinkle with mixed herbs and freshly ground black pepper. *Serves 4–6.*

Mrs Knox's Codling

'Old Mrs Knox received us in the library, where she was seated by a roaring turf fire, which lit the room a good deal more effectively than the pair of candles that stood beside her in tall silver candlesticks. Ceaseless and implacable growls from under her chair indicated the presence of the woolly dog. She talked with confounding culture of the books that rose all round her to the ceiling; her evening dress was accomplished by means of an additional white shawl, rather dirtier than its congeners; as I took her in to dinner she quoted Virgil to me, and in the same breath screeched an objurgation at a being whose head rose suddenly into view from behind an ancient Chinese screen, as I have seen the head of a Zulu woman peer over a bush.'

Experiences of an Irish R.M.

INGREDIENTS
---

36 mussels	8 small onions
2 lb (1 kg) cod	2 oz (50 g) butter, melted
salt and pepper	1 lemon
sprig of thyme	a few fronds of fennel
1 bay leaf	parsley
12 small potatoes	

METHOD

Clean the mussels, put them in a saucepan and cover with water. Cook them, shaking the saucepan to turn them over. When cooked, remove the mussels from their shells and keep them hot. Clean the cod and place in a greased baking tin. Season with salt and pepper, and add thyme and the bay leaf. Parboil the potatoes and put them with the peeled but whole onions around the fish. Pour on the mussel juices and melted butter. Bake in a moderately hot oven 400°F (200°C, gas mark 6), for 20 minutes or until the cod is cooked, basting with the juices every 5 minutes. Serve surrounded by the mussels, garnished with lemon wedges, fennel and parsley. *Serves 6.*

Aussolas Fillet of Sole

'The dining room at Aussolas Castle is one of the many rooms in Ireland in which Cromwell is said to have stabled his horse. On a Louis Quinze chair sat Mrs Knox's woolly dog, its suspicious little eyes peering at her out of their setting of pink lids and dirty white wool. A couple of young horses outside the window tore at the matted creepers on the walls or thrust faces that were half-shy, half-impudent, into the room. Portly pigeons waddled to and fro on the broad window sill, sometimes flying in to perch on the picture frames, while they kept up incessantly a hoarse and pompous cooing.'

Some Experiences of an Irish R.M.

INGREDIENTS
---

4 small or 2 large sole	salt
½ pint (300 ml) milk	2 oz (50 g) butter
6 oz (175 g) grated cheddar cheese	1 oz (25 g) flour
4 egg yolks	3 tablespoons cream
cayenne pepper	2 teaspoons lemon juice

─────────────────────────────METHOD─────────────────────────────

Fillet the sole. Simmer the skin, bones and trimmings in the milk for 5 minutes and then strain the liquid. Mix together 4 oz (100 g) of the cheese and the egg yolks, season with cayenne pepper and salt, spread over the fillets and fold each in half. Place in a shallow, buttered ovenproof dish and bake, covered with buttered paper, in a moderate oven, 350°F (180°C, gas mark 4), for 10 minutes. Meanwhile make a sauce by melting 1 oz (25 g) butter, stirring in the flour, adding the fish cooking milk, and boiling the liquid for 3 minutes. Then add the cream, lemon juice and a further ounce (25 g) of cheese. Pour the sauce over the fish, sprinkle the remaining cheese on top, dot with the rest of the butter, and brown quickly under the grill. *Serves 4.*

Yokahn Herring

One night to the rocks of Yokahn
Came the barque *Isabella* so dandy,
To pieces she went before dawn,
Herself and her cargo of brandy,
And all met a wathery grave
Excepting the vessels's carpenther,
Poor fellow, so far from his home.

Some Experiences of an Irish R.M.

─────────────────────────────INGREDIENTS─────────────────────────────

1 lb (450 g) herrings, filleted
French mustard
salt and pepper
1 oz (25 g) butter
1½ lb (700 g) potatoes, sliced

1 large cooking apple, sliced
1 large onion, sliced
1 tablespoon chopped parsley
lemon juice

─────────────────────────────METHOD─────────────────────────────

Spread the fillets of herring with mustard, season with salt and pepper and roll up. Butter an ovenproof dish and lay half the potatoes in it, then half the apple and onion. Place the herring rolls on top, then sprinkle with parsley and lemon juice. Lay the rest of the onion, apple and potatoes on top. Pour in enough boiling water to come half way up the dish, dot with the rest of the butter and season well. Cover and bake in a moderate oven, 350°F (180°C, gas mark 4) for 30 minutes or so. Uncover and turn up the oven to 400°F (200°C, gas mark 6) for another 30 minutes. *Serves 4.*

Brill in a Blanket

────────────────────INGREDIENTS────────────────────

8 large, tender lettuce leaves   *For the sauce*
4 fillets of brill   2 eggs
salt and pepper   ¼ pint (150 ml) fish stock (page 109)
lemon juice
2 oz (50 g) peeled, cooked shrimps
1 oz (25 g) butter
2 tablespoons white wine

────────────────────METHOD────────────────────

Blanch the lettuce leaves for 2 minutes in boiling salted water. Drain.
Season the fillets of brill with salt and pepper and a squeeze of lemon
juice. In the centre of each place a few shrimps, also seasoned. Roll up
the fillets. Arrange the lettuce leaves in pairs, overlapping each other.
Place a rolled fillet in the centre of each pair and roll the lettuce around
each. Squeeze gently in the hand to make a parcel. Melt the butter in a
shallow pan, put in the wine and the parcels and cook gently for 30
minutes, covered. Remove from the pan and keep warm whilst
preparing the sauce.

    To make the sauce, beat the eggs, add the fish stock and a squeeze
more of lemon juice. Stir this into the buttery juices remaining in the
pan over a moderate heat until the sauce has heated through and
thickened slightly. *Serves 4.*

Headfirst Mackerel

An old Irish tradition says that mackerel, herring and pilchard must be
eaten starting at the head end and finishing with the tail. A failure to
follow this means the fish turn tail and leave the fishing waters,
depriving local fishermen of another catch. One way to get around any
unpleasant consequences of this tradition is to fillet the fish!

---INGREDIENTS---

4 mackerel
butter for greasing
lemon juice
salt and pepper
2 bay leaves
12 peppercorns

4 cloves
1 onion, finely sliced
water and white wine vinegar
shredded lettuce and horseradish
sauce (page 111)

---METHOD---

Clean and wash the mackerel. Place them in a greased ovenproof dish and sprinkle with lemon juice. Add the herbs, seasonings and sliced onion. Cover with equal quantities of water and vinegar. Put a lid on and place in the oven at 400°F (200°C, gas mark 6), for 40 minutes. Once they are cooked, allow them to cool. Lift out the fish and place on a bed of shredded lettuce. Serve with horseradish sauce, mellowed with the addition of a few tablespoons of double cream. *Serves 4.*

VEGETABLES

Paddy's Cheese and Potato Pie

———————————INGREDIENTS———————————

5 large potatoes
2 oz (50 g) butter
salt and pepper

2 eggs, separated
4 oz (100 g) grated cheese
1 tablespoon chopped parsley

———————————METHOD———————————

Cook and then mash the potatoes, while they are still hot, with the butter, season with salt and pepper and mix together with the egg yolks. Add 2 tablespoons of the grated cheese and the chopped parsley. Beat the egg whites until stiff peaks form and fold in. Sprinkle the rest of the cheese on top and bake in a buttered ovenproof dish, in a moderate oven, 350°F (180°C, gas mark 4), for about 20 minutes. *Serves 4.*

Champ

Champ is the most popular potato dish in Ireland. Mrs Cadogan's mother would serve it every Friday. She would boil up some potatoes and then pound them with a beetle. Her husband would then be summoned and as he pounded the potatoes, his wife would add spring onions and chives. He would beetle it until it was smooth as butter.

While pounding he would sing:

> There was an old woman
> Who lived in a lamp
> She had no room
> To beetle her champ.
> She's up with the beetle
> And broke the lamp
> And then she had room
> To beetle her champ.

─────────────────INGREDIENTS─────────────────

2 lb (1 kg) potatoes
4 oz (100 g) chopped spring onion
8 fl oz (225 ml) hot milk

salt and pepper
about 5 tablespoons melted butter

─────────────────METHOD─────────────────

Boil and then mash the potatoes. Simmer the spring onions in the milk for 5 minutes or so; drain but reserve the milk. Season the mashed potatoes to taste, then add the spring onions and beat in enough hot milk to make the mash light, fluffy and smooth. Put into a shallow serving dish. To eat, put a good dollop on your plate. Make a well in the centre and pour in some melted butter. Eat from the outside of the champ and dip each forkful in the golden lake of butter. For variety, use cooked peas or diced carrots or chopped cabbage instead of spring onions. *Serves 4.*

Whipped Potatoes

'The Irish have several ways of eating potatoes: the poorer sort eat them with salt only after they are boiled, others with butter and salt, but most with milk and sugar. Also where they can get a piece of pork, bacon or saltbeef they account it excellent with boiled potatoes'. This was written in 1744. Over 150 years later, Mrs Cadogan's favourite potato dish was whipped potato.

─────────────────INGREDIENTS─────────────────

1 lb (500 g) potatoes
1 oz (25 g) butter
½ pint (300 ml) milk

nutmeg
salt and pepper

——————————————METHOD——————————————

Peel the potatoes and simmer them for 30 minutes. Bring the butter and milk to the boil and add the potatoes. Whip them well together with a wooden spoon; add nutmeg and seasoning to taste and serve. *Serves 2.*

Colcannon

Colcannon is eaten every year in Ireland on Hallowe'en night. It is so good, it should be eaten more often.

> Did you ever eat colcannon
> when 'twas made with thickened cream,
> And the greens and scallions blended
> Like the pictures in a dream?
>
> ˙Did you ever make a hole on top
> To hide the melting cake
> Of clover-flavoured butter
> Which your mother used to make?
>
> Did you ever eat, and eat afraid
> You'd let the ring go past.
> And some old married spinster
> Would get it at the last?

The last verse of this traditional rhyme refers to the old custom of putting a wedding ring in the colcannon. If the ring ended on the plate of a young girl, she would surely marry during the following year.

——————————————INGREDIENTS——————————————

8 medium potatoes	salt and pepper
1 lb (450 g) kale or cabbage	2 oz (50 g) butter
½ pint (300 ml) creamy milk	2 tablespoons chopped parsley

——————————————METHOD——————————————

Peel the potatoes and boil in salted water until tender. Shred the kale or cabbage finely and boil rapidly in a little salted water, turning occasionally. Mash the potatoes. Heat the creamy milk and mix into the potatoes. Stir in the kale or cabbage. Season well. Blend over a low flame until the mixture is green in colour and fluffy in texture. Just before serving, melt the butter, hollow out the centre of the mixture and pour it in. Scatter the chopped parsley over. *Serves 4.*

Buttered Celery

--------INGREDIENTS--------

1 head of celery
2 oz (50 g) butter

salt and pepper

--------METHOD--------

Wash the celery sticks and cut each one into 4 pieces. Melt the butter in an ovenproof dish and put in the celery and seasoning. Cook in a moderately hot oven, 400°F (200°C, gas mark 6), for 30 minutes. *Serves 4–6.*

Toasted Parsnips

--------INGREDIENTS--------

1 lb (450 g) parsnips
2 oz (50 g) butter

1 teaspoon brown sugar
black pepper

--------METHOD--------

Peel the parsnips and cut them into 2-inch (5-cm) lengths. Quarter these lengths and boil them in salted water for 15 minutes or until just tender. Drain and dry the parsnips. Melt the butter in a frying pan. Sprinkle the cooked parsnips with brown sugar and put them into the pan. Season them well with freshly ground black pepper and brown all over. *Serves 4.*

Broad Beans with Cream and Tarragon

--------INGREDIENTS--------

2 oz (50 g) butter
1 lb (450 g) shelled broad beans
2 egg yolks
4 tablespoons double cream

juice of ½ lemon
2 teaspoons fresh chopped tarragon
salt and pepper

--------METHOD--------

Melt the butter in a saucepan, add the beans and a ladleful or so of water, cover and cook very gently until the beans are tender (10–20 minutes, the cooking time will depend on the age of the beans). Shake the pan occasionally so that the beans do not stick. Beat the egg yolks and the cream together and add lemon juice, salt and pepper and tarragon. Stir this sauce into beans. Do not boil but just heat. *Serves 6.*

Cabbage Roll

---INGREDIENTS---

1 large head of cabbage	1 onion, diced
2 oz (50 g) butter	1 red pepper, finely chopped
1 oz (25 g) flour	1 clove garlic, crushed
¼ pint (150 ml) milk	salt and pepper
4 oz (100 g) cooked rice	¼ pint (150 ml) stock
8 oz (225 g) chopped cooked ham	

---METHOD---

Remove the leaves from the cabbage and blanch 8 large ones by putting them in boiling water for 2 minutes. Melt the butter and mix it with the flour, gradually add the milk and bring to the boil. Add the rice, the ham, the onion, red pepper the crushed garlic and the seasoning. Spread out the cabbage leaves one by one, place a spoonful of the stuffing in the centre of each and roll up, tucking in the ends. Place in a casserole dish. Pour in the stock and cook for 30 minutes in a medium oven, 350°F (180°C, gas mark 4). *Serves 4.*

Dry White Cabbage

---INGREDIENTS---

1 medium-sized white cabbage	1–2 tablespoons white wine vinegar
a little olive oil	salt and pepper
1 small onion, chopped	1 tablespoon caster sugar
2–3 large tomatoes, skinned and chopped	

---METHOD---

Discard the outer leaves of the cabbage, remove the hard part of the stalk and cut the leaves into fine strips. Heat a little olive oil in a large, heavy saucepan and soften the onion in it for about 5 minutes. Add the tomatoes and cook until they too are soft, about 10 minutes. Then add the cabbage, wine vinegar and seasoning to taste. Simmer, stirring often, for about 20 minutes over a low heat. Five minutes before serving, stir in the caster sugar. *Serves 4.*

Tomatoes and Cucumbers with Herbs

──────────────INGREDIENTS──────────────

1 cucumber
4 firm tomatoes
½ lemon
2 tablespoons each chopped chives
   and parsley

1 egg
½ teaspoon mustard
salt and pepper
4 fl oz (100 ml) oil

──────────────METHOD──────────────

Peel the cucumber, cut it in half lengthways and scoop out the seedy centre; dice the flesh. Cut the tomatoes in quarters, remove the seeds and dice the flesh also.

Squeeze the juice from the lemon and prepare the herbs. Separate the egg and put the yolk into a small bowl with the mustard and a little salt and pepper. Beat in the oil little by little, beating all the time, then stir in the herbs and lemon juice.

Place the prepared cucumber and tomato in a salad bowl, add the mayonnaise and toss well. *Serves 4.*

Franco-Hibernian Beans

──────────────INGREDIENTS──────────────

1 lb (450 g) French beans
3 tablespoons olive oil
2 onions, thinly sliced
2 tomatoes, skinned, seeded and
   chopped

2 tablespoons chopped parsley
salt and freshly ground black pepper

──────────────METHOD──────────────

Boil the French beans in water for 5–10 minutes until just tender; drain them.

Heat the oil in a frying pan and sauté the sliced onion in it until it turns pale gold. Add the tomatoes and beans and cook with the onions for 10 minutes. Add the chopped parsley, salt and pepper, stir over a low heat for a few minutes and serve right away. *Serves 4.*

Tiny Braised Onions

---INGREDIENTS---

2 lb (1 kg) small onions, peeled
4 oz (100 g) butter
1 teaspoon sugar

1 teaspoon salt
freshly ground black pepper
juice of 1 lemon

---METHOD---

Put the onions into a shallow, ovenproof dish. Cut the butter into little pieces and place evenly over the onions; sprinkle with salt, sugar, plenty of black pepper and the lemon juice. Cover with foil and a lid and cook in a moderate oven, 350°F (180°C, gas mark 4) for 30 minutes or until just tender. Check the vegetables from time to time to make sure they do not stick or scorch, and lower the oven heat if necessary. *Serves 4.*

Master Eddy's Carrot Sticks

---INGREDIENTS---

1 lb (450 g) carrots
1 oz (25 g) butter
salt and pepper
pinch of sugar

2 tablespoons finely chopped
    parsley
6 tablespoons double cream
2 egg yolks

---METHOD---

Cut the carrots into thin, narrow sticks. Put them into a heavy based saucepan with a few tablespoons of water, the butter, seasonings, and chopped parsley. Cook gently for 10 minutes or so. When the carrots are still crisp, stir in the cream and continue to cook slowly until tender. At this stage, stir a little of the cooking liquid into the egg yolks and pour this into the pan. Stir thoroughly, heat through, without boiling, and serve right away. *Serves 4.*

SAVOURIES AND SMALL SUPPERS

Mascallach Ramekins

In west Cork on Hallowe'en night, the children dress up in ghostly clothes and masks and go in groups to all the local houses. They knock on the doors and are given entrance. Then they sing a song:

> God bless the lady of this house
> With the golden chain around her neck
> And if she do fall sick or sore
> The Lord to her her health restore.

The household always gives the children money. Philippa Yeates, who couldn't resist this sort of thing and was always deeply touched, would give the children these ramekins as well.

---INGREDIENTS---

12 oz (350 g) mushrooms
2 oz (50 g) butter
salt and cayenne pepper
1 teaspoon flour

¼ pint (150 ml) soured cream
1 oz (25 g) gruyère or parmesan
  cheese, grated

---METHOD---

Sauté the mushrooms in half the butter for a few minutes. Season to taste. Sprinkle the flour over, cook a few more minutes, stirring, then add the soured cream. Bring to the boil, then pour the mixture into 4 ramekins or small gratin dishes. Melt the rest of the butter and pour it over the top. Sprinkle with the grated cheese and bake in a moderately hot oven, 400°F (200°C, gas mark 6) until the top is golden and bubbling. *Serves 4.*

Coriander Mushrooms

---------------------------------INGREDIENTS---------------------------------

1 lb (450 g) mushrooms   juice of 1 lemon
2 shallots or 1 small onion   4 sprigs parsley
1 clove garlic   3 tablespoons oil
5 coriander seeds

---------------------------------METHOD---------------------------------

Wash the mushrooms (in a bowl of water with a little vinegar added; it will help stop them discolouring); then dry and slice them finely and place in a salad bowl.

Chop finely the shallots or small onion and garlic and add to the mushrooms and the coriander and pour over the lemon juice. Salt lightly but grind over plenty of black pepper. Chill for several hours if possible.

When about to serve, chop the parsley. Sprinkle the oil over the mushrooms, scatter over the parsley and mix through well. *Serves 4.*

Musheggs

'No, darling, *not* with an egg!' replied Philippa, removing the honey spoon from the grasp of her youngest child, just too late to arrest disaster; 'we *don't* eat honey with eggs'.

Further Experiences of an Irish R.M.

---------------------------------INGREDIENTS---------------------------------

6 hard-boiled eggs   2 oz (50 g) grated Irish cheddar
8 oz (225 g) mushrooms
½ pint (300 ml) white sauce (see
    page 110)

---------------------------------METHOD---------------------------------

Shell the hard-boiled eggs, cut them in half lengthwise. Remove yolks, which are to be chopped up finely with the mushrooms and mixed with a few spoonfuls of white sauce. Fill the egg whites with this mixture. Cover the eggs thinly with white sauce, sprinkle with grated cheese and brown slightly in a moderate oven, 375°F (190°C, gas mark 5). *Serves 6.*

Mrs Coffey's Salmon Livers on Toast

————————————————INGREDIENTS————————————————

1 oz (25 g) butter
4 salmon livers

4 slices hot brown toast
freshly ground black pepper

————————————————METHOD————————————————

Melt the butter and gently fry the salmon livers in it for 2 minutes. Serve on slices of toast and pour the excess butter on top. Finish with a grinding of fresh black pepper. *Serves 4.*

Cod's Roe on Toast

Cod's roe is a traditional breakfast dish in Ireland. Major Yeates, however, true to the preferences of his own country, preferred his roes in the form of an after-dinner savoury like this one.

————————————————INGREDIENTS————————————————

8 oz (225 g) cooked cod's roe
3 oz (75 g) breadcrumbs
nutmeg
salt and pepper
2 tablespoons chopped parsley

juice of ½ lemon
2 eggs, separated
4 tablespoons double cream
4 slices white bread, crusts removed
1 oz (25 g) butter

————————————————METHOD————————————————

Cut the cooked cod's roe into slices and mix with the breadcrumbs, nutmeg, salt and pepper. Add the parsley, lemon juice and egg yolks beaten up with the cream. Set aside for 10 minutes or so. Meanwhile stiffly beat the egg whites and toast the slices of bread, buttering them while still warm. Fold the beaten egg whites into the cod's roe mixture, divide this among the slices of toast and bake in a moderately hot oven, 400°F (200°C, gas mark 6) for 15 minutes or until puffed up and golden brown. *Serves 4.*

Sir Valentine Knox's Creamed Shrimps

---INGREDIENTS---

1 oz (25 g) butter
1 oz (25 g) flour
8 fl oz (250 ml) milk
1 small red pepper, finely chopped
  (optional)
3 oz (75 g) cheddar cheese, grated

4 tablespoons double cream
celery salt
pepper
2 tomatoes, thinly sliced
8 oz (225 g) shrimps

---METHOD---

In a saucepan, melt the butter and stir in the flour. Cook for a few minutes, stirring constantly, then add the milk and whisk over a gentle heat until the sauce is smooth. Add the red pepper, if using, 2 oz (50 g) of the grated cheese, the cream and seasoning to taste. Continue to stir over a gentle heat until the sauce thickens.

Butter 4 ramekins and arrange the sliced tomato in them. Add the prawns, pour the sauce over and sprinkle the tops with the rest of the cheese. Place the ramekins under a grill until golden brown, about 8 minutes. *Serves 4.*

After Dinner Canapés

---INGREDIENTS---

¾ lb (350 g) chicken livers
salt and black pepper
few sprigs of parsley
3 oz (75 g) smoked streaky bacon
1 small onion
2 oz (50 g) butter
4 slices white bread

1 teaspoon each flour and softened
  butter
2 tablespoons cream
1 small glass of port
cayenne pepper
paprika

---METHOD---

Wipe the chicken livers and season them with salt and black pepper. Chop the parsley and dice the bacon. Chop the onion. Melt half the butter in a frying pan and brown the bacon in it, then remove and set aside. Fry the onion in the same fat until golden and then add the liver. Cook them for 7 or 8 minutes, then put in the bacon and stir together over a low heat for a couple of minutes more.

Toast the slices of bread and butter them. Blend together the teaspoon each of flour and butter to a paste. Remove the livers from the pan and slice them finely. Add the flour and butter paste to the pan juices, mix in, with the cream and port, and thicken over a low heat, stirring all the time. Season with a small pinch of cayenne pepper and a big one of paprika.

Arrange the chicken livers on the toast. Put each on a small plate and divide the sauce over them. Sprinkle with parsley and serve hot. *Serves 4.*

Drishane Eggs

---INGREDIENTS---

6 eggs	8 anchovy fillets
2 oz (50 g) butter	chopped parsley
4 slices hot toast	cayenne pepper

---METHOD---

Beat the eggs. Melt the butter and scramble the eggs in it until they are creamy curds. Have ready the hot toast, buttered, and mound the scrambled eggs on top. Place two anchovy fillets on top of each and serve right away, sprinkled with a little finely chopped parsley, and cayenne pepper. *Serves 4.*

Bridgie's Holy Bread

---INGREDIENTS---

For each person	1 teaspoon dripping
	1 egg
1 slice of bread	

---METHOD---

Cut a thick slice of bread and tunnel a small hole in the centre (about 1 inch (2·5 cm) in diameter). Heat the dripping and fry the bread in it. Just as the bread is beginning to crisp, break an egg into the hole. Baste the egg until it is cooked. *Serves 1.*

SWEET DISHES

The Comte de Praline's Fool

'The Comte de Praline in the newest of pink coats and the whitest of breeches, and the most glittering of boots and spurs, stood on the step below Lady Knox, with the bridle of his hireling over his arm, and his shining silk hat in his hand.'

Some Experiences of an Irish R.M.

---INGREDIENTS---

1 lb (450 g) rhubarb
2 oz (50 g) sugar

For the custard
½ pint (300 ml) creamy milk
a good strip of lemon peel

3 large egg yolks
2 tablespoons sugar, or to taste
2 tablespoons rum or brandy (optional)

---METHOD---

Place the rhubarb in a saucepan with ¼ pint (150 ml) water and simmer until tender. Pass through a sieve, mix in the sugar and leave to cool.

Meanwhile, make the egg custard. Scald the milk by bringing it slowly to boiling point with the lemon peel. Cover and leave to steep for 20 minutes or so. Next beat the egg yolks with the sugar (more or less according to the sweetness of your tooth). Strain on the milk slowly, beating well as you do so. Pour this custard mixture into a clean pan and stir over a gentle heat, *without boiling*, until thickened. Taste and sweeten further if you wish, or add a little liquor of your choice – brandy or rum for example. Add the rhubarb purée and refrigerate.
Serves 4.

Blarney Coffee Cream

Cream rich as an Irish brogue,
Coffee strong as a friendly hand,
Sugar sweet as the tongue of a rogue,
Whiskey smooth as the wit of the land.

---INGREDIENTS---

¾ pint (450 ml) milk
2 oz (50 g) coffee beans
4 egg yolks
3 oz (75 g) caster sugar
½ oz (15 g) powdered gelatine

¼ pint (150 ml) double cream,
  lightly whipped
3 egg whites
grated chocolate for decoration

---METHOD---

Prepare a 6 inch (15 cm) soufflé dish and tie a paper collar around it to come 1½ inches (4 cm) above the rim. Scald the milk with the coffee, cover the pan and leave for 20 minutes or so to infuse. Cream the egg yolks and sugar together until light and fluffy, strain on the milk, return to the pan and cook slowly, *without boiling*, until the mixture coats the back of the spoon. Cool. Soak the gelatine in 5 tablespoons water, dissolve over a low heat then add to the cold custard with the whipped cream. When the mixture is beginning to thicken, whisk the egg whites until stiff and fold in. Pour into the soufflé dish and leave in the refrigerator to set. To serve, remove the paper collar and sprinkle with grated chocolate. *Serves 4–6.*

Peter's Almond Pancakes

Peter Cadogan's favourite dish, for he had a sweet tooth, was Almond Pancakes. These would be made by his aunt on Shrove Tuesday, before the dreariness of the Lenten fast.

---INGREDIENTS---

8 pancakes (see page 33)
1½ lb (750 g) dessert apples, peeled,
  cored and sliced
6 tablespoons caster sugar

1½ oz (40 g) ground almonds
juice and grated rind of 3 lemons
½ oz (15 g) arrowroot
icing sugar for dusting

———————————————METHOD———————————————

Make a pancake batter, using the ingredients given in the recipe on page 33, but this time adding a teaspoon of sugar, and fry 8 pancakes. Keep them warm. Poach the apples with 4 tablespoons of the sugar and a tablespoon of water until tender. Mix together the almonds, remaining caster sugar and lemon rind, add them to the apples and stir together lightly. Blend the arrowroot with a little lemon juice. Heat the remaining lemon juice and stir in the arrowroot mixture, boil and simmer for a few minutes. Pour half of this sauce into the apple mixture. Then roll each pancake around a dollop of apple mixture, dust with icing sugar and serve with the remaining sauce. *Serves 4.*

Croquet Pudding

'It must have been nine o'clock before we turned our backs upon the pleasures of the table, and settled back to a hot whisky-punch over a fierce turf fire. Then ensued upon my part one of the most prolonged death-grapples with sleep that it has been my lot to endure. The conversation of Mr. Flynn and his daughters pressed into my brain like a narcotic; after circling heavily round various fashionable topics it settled at length upon croquet, and it was about here that I began to slip from my moorings and drift softly towards unconsciousness. I pulled myself up on the delicious verge of a dream to agree with the statement that "croquet was a fright! You'd boil a leg of mutton while you'd be waiting for your turn!"

'It seemed very long afterwards that the clang of a fire-iron pulled me up with what I fear must have been an audible snort. Old Flynn was standing up in front of the fire; he had obviously reached the climax of a narrative, he awaited my comment. "That-that must have been very nice", I said desperately. "Nice!" echoed Mr Flynn, and his astounded face shocked me into consciousness; "sure she might have burned the house down!"'

Further Experiences of an Irish R.M.

———————————————INGREDIENTS———————————————

24 large apricots	*Crumble topping*
sugar to taste	5 oz (150 g) flour
2 oz (50 g) slivered almonds	2 oz (50 g) caster sugar
	4 oz (100 g) butter

If the apricot skins are a little tough, peel them first, otherwise simply quarter and stone them. Arrange in a shallow baking dish and sprinkle with sugar.

Prepare the crumble topping. Sift the flour, stir in the sugar and then add the butter, cutting it in with a knife. When the pieces are quite small, rub them in with your fingertips. Spoon this topping over the apricots, sprinkle the slivered almonds over and bake in a moderate oven, 375°F (190°C, gas mark 5) for 25–30 minutes or until crisp and golden. Serve with cream or custard (page 96). *Serves 4–6.*

Matrimonial Soufflé

Major Yeates knew that the Irish character either loves food best, or drink best, or both equally. The Major himself subscribed to the view that soup and fish explain half the emotions of life, but thought none the worse of a man like Slipper, for whom food is something you choose to go with porter, never the other way around. Slipper would agree with an old Irish saying that there are only two things in the world too serious to be jested on – 'potatoes and matrimony'.

INGREDIENTS

3 whole eggs and 2 yolks
2 oz (50 g) caster sugar
½ oz (15 g) powdered gelatine
juice of 2 lemons
¼ pint (150 ml) tinned pineapple juice
¼ pint (150 ml) whipped cream

For filling
1 medium pineapple
kirsch
caster sugar
halved red and green glacé cherries (optional)

METHOD

Prepare a 6-inch (15-cm) soufflé dish and set a small jam jar, lightly oiled, in the centre. Place the eggs and egg yolks in a bowl, add the sugar and whisk over gentle heat until thickened. Remove from the heat and whisk until cool. Soften the gelatine in 2 tablespoons of water and then dissolve over gentle heat in the lemon juice. Add to the mixture with the pineapple juice. Stir over ice until thickening, then fold in the whipped cream. Turn into the soufflé dish and leave to set.

To finish, peel and slice the pineapple and sprinkle it with kirsch and sugar. When the soufflé is set, remove the jar and fill the centre with the prepared pineapple and a few glacé cherries. *Serves 4–6.*

John Cullinane's Ice Cream

John Cullinane, a local farmer, came to call at Shreelane to talk to the Major about a horse. The R.M. was delayed at Court, but Philippa made the man welcome and offered him some tea. The farmer was well used to porter, but had never had tea. He did not like to offend, and so said yes, thanking his honour's ladyship, tea would do him very well.

The tea arrived and was poured. Philippa handed the baffled farmer a delicate little cup and saucer filled with greenish liquid saying, 'There you are, Mr Cullinane, sweeten it to your liking'. At that moment she was called out of the room, and so did not see the grimace of displeasure on the poor man's face as he sipped the bitter liquid.

A few months later, the man returned again to find the Major absent. To his horror, Philippa offered him tea, and again he could not refuse. This time Philippa put some sugar in the tea before giving it to him. It was with a sinking heart that the brave farmer sipped the liquid, but to his amazement it was delicious, not at all bitter. Philippa saw the look of delight on his face as he sipped the tea.

'Ah, Mr Cullinane', she said, 'it is very nice to see an Irishman who really appreciates tea'.

'It is tea I like to be sure, ma'am', he replied 'but I'm not enjoying the drink they call "sweeten-it-to-your-liking".'

―――――――――――――――――INGREDIENTS―――――――――――――――――

1 pint (600 ml) double cream   4 oz (100 g) caster sugar
4 well beaten egg yolks
½ pint (300 ml) cold Indian tea (very
   strong)

―――――――――――――――――METHOD―――――――――――――――――

Scald the cream over a low heat. Remove from the heat, stir in the tea, sugar and beaten egg yolks. Stir all the time over a very low heat until the mixture begins to thicken. Sieve and freeze. *Serves 4–6.*

Irish Storyteller's Ice Cream

There are two Irish proverbs which, by their accuracy, trap the storyteller in an agony of indecision. One says 'A drink before a story', while the other replies 'A drink is shorter than a story'. This liqueur ice cream should be served at the beginning of a story, and is almost certain to last until the end.

─────────────── INGREDIENTS ───────────────

3 bananas
3 oz (75 g) walnuts
2 oz (50 g) caster sugar
½ pint (300 ml) whipped cream

6 tablespoons Jameson's Irish Velvet
    Irish coffee liqueur
3 egg whites

─────────────── METHOD ───────────────

Slice the bananas and chop the walnuts. Mix them together with the sugar, cream and 2 tablespoons of the liqueur. Beat the egg whites until soft peaks form and fold into the mixture. Freeze the mixture, either in a machine or by using ice trays. Arrange for serving as desired, and spoon 1 teaspoon of liqueur over each of the portions. *Serves 6.*

Tomsy Flood's Chocolate Pudding

'"Ah, poor Tomsy! He took to this, y'know," Miss Bennett slightly jerked her little finger, "and he wouldn't ride a donkey over a sod of turf. They sent him out to South Africa, to an ostrich farm, and when the people found he couldn't ride they put him to bed with a setting of ostrich eggs to keep them warm, and he did that grand, till someone gave him a bottle of whisky, he got rather lively and broke all the eggs. They say it's a lay-preacher he's going to be now!".'

In Mr Knox's Country

─────────────── INGREDIENTS ───────────────

3 eggs
8 oz (225 g) plain chocolate

3 tablespoons sugar
8 trifle sponges

─────────────── METHOD ───────────────

Separate the eggs. Melt the chocolate with 3 tablespoons of water and cool. Beat the sugar and egg yolks in a double saucepan. Add the chocolate. Beat the egg whites and fold them in. Lay the sponges in a glass dish, cover with the chocolate mixture and chill. *Serves 4.*

Sally's Lemon Syllabub

--------------------------INGREDIENTS--------------------------

4 fl oz (100 ml) white wine or sherry   2 oz (50 g) caster sugar
2 small lemons   ½ pint (300 ml) double cream

----------------------------METHOD----------------------------

Mix the wine or sherry with the grated rind and juice of the lemons.
Stir in the sugar until it dissolves. Still stirring, pour in the cream
slowly. Beat the syllabub with a whisk until it holds its shape – be
careful about this because if you beat too long the mixture will curdle.
Serves 4–6.

Fudge Pudding

--------------------------INGREDIENTS--------------------------

4 oz (100 g) butter   2 oz (50 g) flour
4½ oz (115 g) caster sugar   ½ teaspoon vanilla essence
2 eggs, separated   pinch salt
2 oz (50 g) grated chocolate   butter for greasing

----------------------------METHOD----------------------------

Beat the butter until soft, add the caster sugar and beat until creamy.
Beat in the egg yolks. Melt the chocolate over hot water and when
slightly cool, add to the mixture. Sift the flour and beat it in, adding the
vanilla essence. Whip the egg whites with a pinch of salt until stiff.
Fold into the mixture. Bake in a 7-inch (17·5-cm) shallow greased pie
dish in a moderate oven, 350°F (180°C, gas mark 4), for about 35
minutes. Serve topped with ice cream or whipped cream. *Serves 3.*

Arbutus Tartlets

Philippa and Sinclair Yeates spent a short late-autumn holiday in
Killarney, with Sally Knox. One day they made an expedition to Lough
Leane, where Philippa was intrigued by this shrub, with its vibrant,
dark-red fruits. She picked some and took them back to Shreelane,
where Mrs Cadogan filled little tartlets with them. Failing arbutus,
redcurrants and raspberries would make a fine substitute.

INGREDIENTS

Rich shortcrust pastry
4 oz (100 g) flour
pinch of salt
1 tablespoon caster sugar
2 oz (50 g) softened butter
1 small egg

Filling
12 oz (350 g) arbutus
redcurrant jelly
caster sugar

METHOD

Sift the flour onto the work surface. Make a well in the centre and put in the salt, sugar, butter and egg. Gradually blend in the flour with your fingers, then quickly mix to a dough. Chill for 30 minutes at least before using.

Roll out the dough and line 6 3-inch (7·5-cm) tartlet tins using it. Line with foil, weight with dried beans and bake in a 375°F (190°C, gas mark 5) oven for 12–15 minutes. Remove the paper and beans after 8–10 minutes.

Fill the tartlets just before serving, if possible. Prepare the arbutus and brush the pastry shells with redcurrant jelly. Fill with the fruit, sprinkle lightly with sugar and brush over the top with a little more warmed redcurrant jelly. *Serves 6.*

Connemara Blackberry and Apple Pie

INGREDIENTS
---

2 lb (1 kg) apples
juice of ½ lemon
1 lb (450 g) blackberries
6–8 oz (175–225 g) sugar

shortcrust pastry made with 4 oz (100 g) flour (page 51)
beaten egg to glaze

METHOD

Peel, core and slice the apples, and sprinkle them with the lemon juice to prevent discolouration. Pack the sliced apples and prepared blackberries in layers in a deep pie dish, sprinkling each layer with plenty of sugar (how much you use will depend on the tartness or otherwise of the apples) and a little nutmeg. Make sure the dish is well filled.

Cover the fruit with a lid of the rolled out shortcrust pastry. Brush the top with beaten egg and put the pie dish into a moderately hot oven, 400°F (200°C, gas mark 6) for about 45 minutes. Exactly how much time the cooking takes will depend on the depth of your dish but it is done when a sharp pointed knife pierces the apple easily. If the pastry crust is getting a little too brown, protect it with buttered greaseproof paper, and turn down the oven heat slightly. Serve with plenty of cream. *Serves 4–6.*

Connaught Trifle

─────────────────────────INGREDIENTS─────────────────────────

6 slices of sponge cake
up to ½ pint (300 ml) sweet white
   wine
¾ pint (450 ml) single cream
2 large eggs
2 large egg yolks
vanilla sugar
about 8 oz (225 g) fresh raspberries *or*
   raspberry or strawberry jam

2 tablespoons brandy
juice of 1 lemon
½ pint (300 ml) double cream
toasted slivered almonds and
   angelica for decoration

─────────────────────────METHOD─────────────────────────

Put the slices of sponge cake in the bottom of a wide glass bowl. Pour over the wine and leave it to soak in.

Make the next layer, the custard, by first bringing the single cream up to a boil. Beat the eggs and egg yolks together, pour the scalded cream over them, whisking as you do so, and stir over a low heat until it thickens sufficiently to coat the back of a spoon. Be very careful not to let the custard mixture come to a boil for this would curdle and ruin it. Sweeten to taste with vanilla sugar and leave to cool.

While the custard is cooling, purée the raspberries, sweeten them to taste and spread over the sponge cake layer. If you are using jam, simply spread a layer of this over the cake; keep it thin.

Spoon the custard carefully over the fruit or jam.

Put the brandy and lemon juice into a bowl, and slowly pour over the cream, stirring as you do so. Beat until the cream holds its shape. Finally, pile this onto the trifle and decorate as you please with almonds and angelica. *Serves 8–10.*

Plum Puff

For Mrs Cadogan to make this for nursery tea was the greatest treat Major and Mrs Yeates' small sons could imagine.

──────────────────────────INGREDIENTS──────────────────────────

about 1 lb (450 g) plums
8 oz (225 g) puff pastry
about 3 oz (150 g) roughly chopped
   walnuts (optional)

sugar
beaten egg to glaze

──────────────────────────METHOD──────────────────────────

Halve the plums and remove their stones.

Roll out the pastry into 2 squares measuring about 7 inches (17 cm). Dampen a baking sheet and place one square upon it. Brush a wide band around the edge with water and place the plums, cut side down, in the centre. Sprinkle with sugar, and the walnuts too if you have them.

Fold the other square of pastry in half. Using a sharp knife, cut a series of slits in the pastry, leaving a rim. Open out the cut pastry and lift it onto the fruit and the other square of pastry. Press the edges firmly together. Brush the pastry with beaten egg and bake in a hot oven, 425°F (220°C, gas mark 7) until golden brown, about 25 minutes.

If the pastry seems to be browning too much or too quickly, lower the oven heat and protect the top with dampened greaseproof paper. *Serves 4.*

Iced Raspberry Soufflé

──────────────────────────INGREDIENTS──────────────────────────

1 lb (450 g) fresh raspberries
4 eggs, separated
about 8 oz (225 g) caster sugar
1 tablespoon kirsch

½ pint (300 ml) double cream
2 teaspoons powdered gelatine
2 tablespoons grated chocolate

──────────────────────────METHOD──────────────────────────

Keep back a few of the best raspberries for decoration. Push the rest through a fine sieve.

Place the egg yolks into a saucepan with the sugar and raspberry puŕe and whisk over a low heat until it becomes thick and frothy. Add the kirsch.

Whip the cream until it holds its shape, and fold two-thirds of it into the raspberry mixture.

Dissolve the gelatine in 4 tablespoons water over low heat, add to the mousse mixture and stir, over ice, until it begins to set.

Whip the egg whites until stiff, fold them into the mousse and put into a soufflé dish. leave to chill until set. When ready to serve, decorate with the reserved raspberries and cream, and grated chocolate. *Serves 4.*

Philippa's Pear Pie

---INGREDIENTS---

rich shortcrust pastry made with 4 oz (100 g) flour (page 96)
4 pears
juice of ½ lemon
8 fl oz (250 ml) double cream

2 small egg yolks
2 tablespoons syrup from preserved ginger
3 knobs preserved ginger, chopped

---METHOD---

Roll out the pastry and line a tart tin about 8 inches (20 cm) in diameter. Line with foil and fill with dried beans and bake in a moderately hot oven 400°F (200°C, gas mark 6) for 10–15 minutes until golden.

Peel and core the pears and, if they are ripe, simply sprinkle with lemon juice to keep them from discolouring. If they are a little on the hard side, poach them lightly first. Whichever you decide to do first, next slice the pears and arrange them neatly in the pastry shell.

Beat together the cream and egg yolks. Sweeten this to taste with the ginger syrup. Stir in the chopped preserved ginger. Pour this over the pears and put back into the oven. Reduce the heat to moderate, 375°F (190°C, gas mark 5), and cook until just set, about 25 minutes or so. *Serves 4–6.*

BREAD AND CAKES

Traditional Soda Bread

---INGREDIENTS---

¾ teaspoon bicarbonate of soda
6 oz (175 g) white plain flour
1 teaspoon salt

10 oz (275 g) wholemeal flour
about ½ pint (300 ml) buttermilk

---METHOD---

Get rid of any lumps in the bicarbonate of soda. Sieve the soda, white flour and the salt into a bowl and mix in the wholemeal flour.

Make a well in the centre of the mixture and put in the buttermilk. Mix to a soft dough, turn out onto a floured surface and knead until the side next to the work surface is smooth. Turn it smooth side up, shape it into a round, flatten it out slightly and cut a cross in the top with a floured knife. Place the bread dough on a lightly floured baking sheet and bake in a fairly hot oven 375°F (190°C, gas mark 5) for about 40 minutes. The loaf is ready when it sounds hollow when tapped on the base with the knuckles. Turn out of the tin and leave to cool, wrapped in a cloth. Serve while fresh.

Note: If you have not any buttermilk to hand, this bread can be made with ordinary milk; in this case you would need to add 2 teaspoons cream of tartar with the bicarbonate of soda.

Guinness Plum Cake

Extract from *The History of Saint James's Gate Brewery*.

'It would appear from evidence collected and facts ascertained after the most careful enquiry that Guinness Extra Stout has been found most useful in the following types of cases:

1 Dyspepsia: As a tonic and stomachic in cases of sluggish action of the alimentary canal, Extra Stout has often had a wonderful effect.
2 Insomnia: The soporific effects of Extra Stout are sometimes remarkable, and doctors have declared that it is preferable to Opium, inducing a more natural and healthy sleep, while avoiding the establishment of a drug habit.
3 General Debility: Convalescence after long or acute illness, when vitality is low, sleep disturbed, digestion impaired and nerves are in a state of irritability, the vitalising properties of Extra Stout have proved to be of immense help.'

---INGREDIENTS---

8 oz (225 g) butter
1 lb (500 g) flour
2 oz (50 g) brown sugar
8 oz (225 g) sultanas
8 oz (225 g) currants
4 oz (100 g) chopped candied peel

1 dessertspoon cinnamon
grated rind of 1 lemon
3 eggs, beaten
1 tablespoon bicarbonate of soda
½ pint (300 ml) Guinness

---METHOD---

Rub the butter into the flour, add the sugar, dried fruit, peel, cinnamon and lemon rind. Add the eggs and the bicarbonate of soda to the Guinness. Beat for one minute and add to the other ingredients, mixing thoroughly. Turn into a greased and prepared 8-inch (20-cm) tin and bake for 1½ to 2 hours at 325°F (170°C, gas mark 3). Store in an airtight tin for two weeks before eating.

Mrs Cadogan's Christmas Cake

While Mrs Cadogan mixed her famous cake, she would sing the sad story of Mrs Houligan's Christmas Cake:

> There was plums and prunes and cherries
> And citrons and raisins and cinnamon too,
> There was nutmeg and cloves and berries,
> And the top it was nailed on with glue.
> There was caraway seeds in abundance,
> T'would build up a fine stomach-ache,
> You'd kill a man twice after eating one slice
> Of Mrs Houligan's Christmas Cake.

──────────────────INGREDIENTS──────────────────

14 oz (400 g) currants or raisins
1 lb (450 g) sultanas
4 oz (100 g) mixed peel
4 oz (100 g) glacé cherries
1 tablespoon brandy or rum
grated rind and juice of 1 lemon
grated rind and juice of 1 orange

8 oz (225 g) brown sugar
8 oz (225 g) butter
10 oz (275 g) plain flour
1 oz (25 g) ground almonds
5 large eggs
2 teaspoons mixed spice

──────────────────METHOD──────────────────

Prepare the fruit mixture a day ahead by mixing together: the currants (or raisins), sultanas, mixed peel and cherries with the brandy or rum, orange and lemon rind and juice. Mix thoroughly, cover and leave overnight.

Cream together until light the brown sugar, butter, 2 oz (50 g) of the flour and the ground almonds. Then add eggs one at a time, making sure each one has been thoroughly mixed before adding the next. (Flour and ground almonds prevent eggs from curdling.) When the eggs are in, add the remaining flour and the spices gently. Lastly add the fruit which has been prepared beforehand. Put into a greased and lined 8 inch (20 cm) square cake tin. Bake for 4 hours at 300°F (150°C, gas mark 3).

Flurry and Sally's Wedding Cake

'We fetched the bride and bridegroom from the church; we fetched old Eustace Hamilton, who married them; we dug out the champagne from the cellar; we even found rice and threw it.

'The hired carriage that had been ordered to take the runaways across country to a distant station was driven by Slipper. He was shaved; he wore an old livery coat and a new pot hat; he was wondrous sober. On the following morning he was found asleep on a heap of stones ten miles away; somewhere in the neighbourhood one of the horses was grazing in a field with a certain amount of harness hanging about it. The carriage and the remaining horse were discovered in a roadside ditch, two miles farther on; one of the carriage doors had been torn off, and in the interior the hens of the vicinity were conducting an exhaustive search after the rice that lurked in the cushions.'

Some Experiences of an Irish R.M.

INGREDIENTS

8 oz (225 g) plain flour
pinch of salt
6 oz (175 g) butter
6 oz (175 g) caster sugar
a few drops vanilla essence
3 eggs
1 tablespoon cocoa powder blended
    with 1–2 tablespoons water

½ teaspoon baking powder
green food colouring

Chocolate icing
8 oz (225 g) cooking chocolate
2 tablespoons milk
knob of butter
thin strips of lemon rind

METHOD

Line and grease an 8-inch (20-cm) deep cake tin. Sift the flour and salt into a bowl. Beat the butter with the sugar until pale and creamy. Add the vanilla essence and beat in the eggs one at a time. Fold in the sifted flour and baking powder.

Put one third of the mixture onto a plate and add the blended cocoa to it. Mix well together.

Take half of the remaining mixture and put it onto another plate. Add the green colouring to it and mix well. Leave the remaining one third plain.

Set the oven at 350°F (180°C, gas mark 4).

Fill the prepared cake tin with alternating colours, one large spoonful at a time, and bake in the heated oven for 1¼ hours. Allow to cool on a wire rack.

To make the icing, melt the chocolate in a small bowl over a saucepan of hot water, add the milk and mix well together. Add the knob of butter and beat until smooth. Pour the chocolate icing over the cake and decorate with lemon strips.

Maria's Poteen Cake

'"Why this dog has taken the most extraordinary fancy to me!" Sybil Hervey (who was really a very amiable girl) would say, and Maria, with a furtive eye upon her owners, would softly draw the guest's third piece of cake into the brown velvet bag she called her mouth.'

Further Experiences of an Irish R.M.

──────────────── INGREDIENTS ────────────────

8 oz (225 g) raisins
8 oz (225 g) sultanas
2 oz (50 g) candied peel
2 oz (50 g) glacé cherries
½ teaspoon mixed spice
1 oz (25 g) chopped almonds
8 fl oz (225 ml) poteen

9 oz (250 g) flour
pinch of salt
6 oz (175 g) butter
6 oz (175 g) caster sugar
1 teaspoon baking powder
2 fl oz (50 ml) milk

──────────────── METHOD ────────────────

Steep the fruit, spices and chopped almonds in poteen (or substitute if poteen is not available) overnight. In the morning sieve the flour and salt, and cream together with the butter and sugar, and add the baking powder and the milk to make a cake mixture.

Mix in the soaked fruit. Put the mixture into a medium-deep greased and lined 8-inch (20-cm) round cake tin and spread out evenly. Cover with greaseproof paper and bake for 2¾ hours in a moderate oven, 350°F (180°C, gas mark 4). When done, leave to cool in the tin. Remove carefully. Wrap and store for 4 days before cutting.

Honey Cakes

'Following the direction of her eyes, I perceived, as it were at the back of the stage, two mysterious, shrouded figures pursuing a swift course towards the house through a shubbery of immense hydrangea bushes. Their heads resembled monster black door-handles, round their shoulders hung flounces of black muslin; in gauntleted hands they bore trays loaded with "sections" of honey; even at a distance of fifty yards we could see their attendant cortège of indignant bees.

'"Taken thirty pounds this morning!" shouted the leading door-handle, speeding towards the house. "Splendid heather honey!"'

In Mr Knox's Country

———————————INGREDIENTS———————————

6 oz (175 g) strong white flour
1 oz (25 g) wheatgerm
½ oz (15 g) coarse bran
1 egg

9 fl oz (250 ml) runny honey
2 oz (50 g) melted butter
pinch of salt

———————————METHOD———————————

Warm the honey slightly. Put all the ingredients together in a basin and beat well. Lightly grease a griddle or heavy-bottomed pan. Drop the mixture in spoonfuls on to it and cook over a moderate heat until browned on both sides. Leave to cool before eating. *Makes about 30.*

The Quaker's (Ginger) Hunting Nuts

'I began to perceive that I had been adopted as a pioneer by a small band of followers who, as one of their number candidly explained, "liked to have someone ahead of them to soften the banks", and accordingly waited respectfully till the Quaker had made the rough places smooth, and taken the raw edges off the walls. They, in their turn, showed me alternative routes when the obstacle proved above the Quaker's limit, thus, in ignoble confederacy, I and the offscourings of the Curranhilty hunt pursued our way across some four miles of country.'

Some Experiences of an Irish R.M.

———————————INGREDIENTS———————————

12 oz (350 g) butter
12 oz (350 g) treacle
12 oz (350 g) caster sugar

12 oz (350 g) medium oatmeal
8 oz (225 g) white flour
½ teaspoon bicarbonate of soda

———————————METHOD———————————

Melt the butter, treacle and sugar together in a saucepan and add the rest of the ingredients. Roll into balls the size of a walnut but slightly flatter. Bake in a moderate oven, 350°F (180°C, gas mark 4) for 12–15 minutes.

Hallowe'en Tea Brack

All Saints Day, November 1st, is a holy day; Hallowe'en is the day before and therefore is a day of abstinence from meat. Tea bread was one of the traditional vegetarian dishes for Hallowe'en. A wedding ring, a small stick, a pea, a bean and a piece of cloth were mixed into the dough before baking. Whoever got the ring would be married within the month. The pea signified poverty, the bean meant riches. With the stick your husband would beat you and the cloth signified that you would never be married.

————————————————INGREDIENTS————————————————

1 lb (450 g) mixed dried fruit
½ pint (300 ml) cold tea
6 oz (175 g) brown sugar
1 lb (450 g) white flour

1 egg, beaten
½ teaspoon mixed spice
2 teaspoons baking powder

————————————————METHOD————————————————

Clean the fruit and steep in the cold tea with the brown sugar for 24 hours. Then add the flour, beaten egg, mixed spice and baking powder. Mix well together, put into a greased 8-inch (20-cm) cake tin, place a round of aluminium foil on top to protect the brack while it is cooking and bake it in a moderate oven 350°F (180°C, gas mark 4), for 2 hours or so. When done it will sound hollow when tapped on the base. If you wish to give the brack the traditional glossy top, brush the top of the finished loaf with a beaten egg mixed with a pinch of salt and return to the oven for 5 minutes.

Boxty

It is possible to cook potatoes very badly, as Major Yeates well knew. It befell him often to spend dreary nights in the dingy hotels of drowsy country towns while taking assizes. When in Court he could readily agree with the judgement of an esteemed Lord Lieutenant of Ireland on the charges of the Irish: 'a decent, kindly, hard-working people but a trifle ingenious in the witness box'. The night before, toying unenthusiastically with hotel-ruined blistered potatoes, the words of Sir Francis Drake echoed with biting irony in his head, 'potatoes be the most delicate roots that may be eaten, and do far exceed parsnips and carrots'. While incarcerated in one of these murky dining-rooms, the Major increasingly sympathised with the view of a foreign philosopher who believed that 'a diet which consists predominantly of potatoes leads to the use of liquor, as does a diet that consists predominantly of rice leads to the use of opium'. These desperate thoughts however, were banished by the elixir, on his return to Shreelane, of Mrs Cadogan's hot Boxty with fresh butter.

──────────────────────── INGREDIENTS ────────────────────────

1 lb (450 g) potatoes	½ teaspoon baking powder
4 oz (100 g) flour	1 egg
1 teaspoon salt	milk
pepper	butter for serving.

──────────────────────── METHOD ────────────────────────

Boil half the potatoes until tender, then mash them; grate the rest of them. Mix the mashed and grated potato, sifted flour, salt, pepper and baking powder into a soft dough with the egg and a little milk if required. Drop tablespoonsful onto a hot griddle or pan and cook over moderate heat until nicely browned on both sides. Serve right away while hot, with lots of butter.

Mrs Knox's Gingerbread

──────────────────────── INGREDIENTS ────────────────────────

4 oz (100 g) butter	12 oz (350 g) flour
4 oz (100 g) brown sugar	1 teaspoon ground ginger
2 eggs	2 oz (50 g) chopped almonds
12 fl oz (350 ml) golden syrup or	1 teaspoon bicarbonate of soda
treacle	2 tablespoons warm milk

──────────────────────── METHOD ────────────────────────

Cream the butter and sugar together. Mix in the eggs and golden syrup or treacle. Sift the flour and ginger together, stir in the chopped almonds then mix into the gingerbread mixture. Stir the bicarbonate of soda into the milk and add in.

Pour the mixture into a 7-inch (15-cm) greased and floured cake tin and bake in a moderate oven, 325°F (160°C, gas mark 3) for 1½ hours, or a little longer if you like a less sticky gingerbread.

Nursery Scones

These tiny scones were the special favourites of both the Masters Yeates.

——————————————INGREDIENTS——————————————

2 oz (50 g) butter
8 oz (225 g) flour
1 tablespoon caster sugar

1 teaspoon salt
milk to mix

——————————————METHOD——————————————

Rub the butter into the flour and mix in the sugar and salt. Mix to a firm dough with a little milk. Knead for a few minutes and then roll out the dough to about ½ inch (1 cm) thick. Cut into small rounds about 1 inch (2·5 cm) or so across. Place on a greased baking sheet and bake in a hot oven, 400°F (200°C, gas mark 6) for 10–15 minutes. *Makes about 20 scones.*

Keeping Chocolate Cake

This extremely good chocolate cake was so named by Mrs Cadogan on account of the fact that it keeps for up to four weeks if stored in an airtight tin.

——————————————INGREDIENTS——————————————

4 oz (100 g) butter
4 oz (100 g) caster sugar
2 eggs, beaten
2 oz (50 g) ground almonds

vanilla essence
2 oz (50 g) grated chocolate
6 oz (175 g) flour
salt

——————————————METHOD——————————————

Line an 8-inch (20-cm) round cake tin with buttered greaseproof paper.

Cream the butter and sugar and add the eggs. Stir in the ground almonds and a few drops of essence. Melt the chocolate in a bowl over hot water and stir it in also. Sift in the flour with a pinch of salt. Beat well.

Pour the mixture into the prepared cake tin and put into a moderate oven, 350°F (180°C, gas mark 4) and bake for 30 minutes. Reduce the oven temperature to 150°F (300°C, gas mark 2) and bake for a further 30 minutes. When the cake is cooked a skewer pushed into the centre will come out clean.

Honey and Orange Thins

──────────────────────INGREDIENTS──────────────────────

4 oz (100 g) butter
8 oz (225 g) flour
pinch of salt

2 tablespoons double cream
2 tablespoons honey
grated rind of 1 orange

──────────────────────METHOD──────────────────────

Rub the butter into the flour and salt. Add the cream, honey and orange rind and work into the dry ingredients with a knife until the mixture holds together. Roll out thinly and cut into small rounds with a cutter. Bake on a greased baking sheet in an oven preheated to 300°F (150°C, gas mark 2) for 15–20 minutes. *Makes about 20.*

Enniscorthy Strawberry Cream Cake

──────────────────────INGREDIENTS──────────────────────

3 eggs
3 oz (75 g) caster sugar
few drops vanilla essence
grated rind of 1 lemon
3 oz (75 g) flour

Filling
1 lb (450 g) strawberries
½ pint (300 ml) double cream

──────────────────────METHOD──────────────────────

Break the eggs into a large bowl. Add the sieved caster sugar, the vanilla essence and lemon rind and whisk until the mixture is thick and creamy. Add in the sieved flour and fold in lightly with a whisk. Line an 8-inch (20-cm) round tin with buttered paper and pour in the mixture. Bake in a moderate oven, 375°F (190°C, gas mark 5) for 15 minutes or so, and then lower the heat to 350°F (180°C, gas mark 4) for a further 15 or 20 minutes. Allow the cake to cool in the tin, then turn it out gently onto a wire rack.

Split the cake horizontally in half. Whip the cream for the filling until it holds its shape. Prepare the fruit, keeping back a handful of the best berries for decoration. Mix the rest of the fruit with the whipped cream and spread over the lower half of the cake. Place the other half gently on top and press down very lightly.

Arrange the reserved strawberries attractively on top of the cake and sprinkle with caster sugar just before serving.

SIMPLE SAUCES FOR ALL OCCASIONS

Simple Poultry or Meat Stock

INGREDIENTS

2 lb (1 kg) boiling fowl or beef bones
  and trimmings
bouquet garni (parsley sprigs, thyme,
  garlic clove, black peppercorns,
  tied in muslin)

1 small onion, unpeeled
1 carrot, sliced
1 stick of celery, sliced

METHOD

Put the boiling fowl or meat bones in a large saucepan. Cover with about 3½ pints (2 litres) cold water and bring slowly to a boil. Skim any fat from the surface. Add the bouquet garni and vegetables. Simmer gently for 2 hours, skimming the surface fat from time to time. Strain the stock and season to taste. Store in the refrigerator for up to 3 days.

Simple Fish Stock

INGREDIENTS

2 lb (1 kg) fish heads, bones and
  trimmings
bouquet garni (parsley sprigs, thyme,
  black peppercorns, tied in muslin)

1 small onion, unpeeled
1 carrot, sliced
1 stick of celery, sliced
1 pint (600 ml) white wine

————————————METHOD————————————

Place the fish, bouquet garni and vegetables in a large pan, add 3½ pints (2 litres) water and bring to the boil over a gentle heat. Skim any scum from the surface as it comes to a simmer and continue to do so until no more scum rises. Cover and simmer for 15 minutes. Add the wine and simmer, covered, for another 15 minutes. Strain and store in the refrigerator for up to 3 days.

White Sauce

————————————INGREDIENTS————————————

1 oz (25 g) butter	salt and white pepper
1 oz (25 g) flour	nutmeg
¾ pint (450 ml) milk	double cream (optional)

————————————METHOD————————————

Melt the butter in a saucepan, mix in the flour and stir over a gentle heat for a few minutes. Add the milk gradually, stirring continuously, and bring to a boil. Simmer for 5 minutes or so until smooth and creamy. Season to taste with salt and white pepper and a grating of nutmeg. Stir in a little double cream if you would like a richer, more velvety sauce.

Brown Sauce

————————————INGREDIENTS————————————

1 onion	1 oz (25 g) flour
1 small carrot	½ pint (300 ml) stock or water
1 oz (25 g) butter or dripping	salt and pepper

————————————METHOD————————————

Chop the onion and carrot and brown them in the butter or dripping, with the flour. Add the stock or water, simmer for 10 minutes, rub through a sieve, season to taste and serve.

Tomato Sauce

---INGREDIENTS---

1 lb (450 g) tomatoes, sliced
½ onion, finely chopped
1 stick of celery, finely chopped
a few leaves of basil or a pinch of
    oregano

a few sprigs of parsley
2 tablespoons olive oil
salt and pepper

---METHOD---

Put all the ingredients into a heavy saucepan and simmer together until the sauce is thick and smooth. Strain through a sieve and serve.

Horseradish Sauce

Mix 2 tablespoons grated horseradish with ½ teaspoon mustard, ½ teaspoon sugar, 2 teaspoons wine vinegar, salt and pepper. Stir carefully into ¼ pint (150 ml) double cream.

Onion Sauce

---INGREDIENTS---

1 large onion
1 oz (25 g) flour
2 oz (50 g) butter

½ pint (300 ml) milk
salt and pepper

---METHOD---

Peel the onion and cut in quarters. Boil in salted water for 10 minutes then chop finely. Simmer in half the butter until soft but not brown.

Meanwhile make a white sauce: melt the remaining butter, add the flour and stir over a gentle heat for a few minutes. Add the milk and bring to a boil, stirring continuously. Boil for 5 minutes, add the cooked onion and simmer again for 5 minutes. Season to taste.

Bread Sauce

―――――――――――――INGREDIENTS―――――――――――――

½ pint (300 ml) milk
1 small onion, stuck with 2 cloves
2 oz (50 g) fresh breadcrumbs
salt and pepper

mace
1 tablespoon butter or double cream
cayenne pepper

―――――――――――――METHOD―――――――――――――

Heat the milk and whole onion with the cloves stuck in it over gentle
heat until it comes just to boiling point. Set aside for 15 minutes or so
to infuse thoroughly. Remove the onion. Whisk in the breadcrumbs,
salt and pepper and a pinch of mace and heat through gently. This
sauce should be neither too thick nor too runny, so add more milk or
breadcrumbs accordingly. Finally, stir in the butter or cream and serve
sprinkled with cayenne pepper.

Cranberry Sauce

―――――――――――――INGREDIENTS―――――――――――――

1 lb (450 g) cranberries
orange juice or water (see below)

about 8 oz (225 g) sugar or to taste

―――――――――――――METHOD―――――――――――――

Put the cranberries into a saucepan, add just enough orange juice or
water to cover and simmer gently for 5–10 minutes or until the berries
pop. Stir in the sugar until dissolved.

Raspberry or Blackberry Vinegar

―――――――――――――INGREDIENTS―――――――――――――

3 lb (1·5 kg) raspberries or
    blackberries

6 pints (3·4 litres) white wine vinegar
sugar

―――――――――――――METHOD―――――――――――――

Pour 2 pints (1·1 litres) of white wine vinegar over 1 lb (500 g) of fruit.
Cover and leave to stand for 4 days. Stir every day. After 4 days, pour
the fruit into a muslin bag and allow the juice to drip through,

unpressured, into a basin. Repeat the process by covering a fresh pound of fruit with the strained liquid. After 4 days, repeat the process once more. Measure the liquid and allow 1 lb (500 g) of sugar to every pint (575 ml). Put the sugar into the preserving pan together with the liquid, boil for 6 minutes and skim on removal from heat. Cool, bottle and cork. Use 1 wine glassful to ½ pint (300 ml) water.

Blackcurrant Vinegar

INGREDIENTS

3 lb (1·5 kg) ripe blackcurrants   3 lb (1·5 kg) sugar
1 pint (600 ml) white wine vinegar

METHOD

Add the vinegar to the blackcurrants and leave for 4 days, stirring daily. After 4 days, boil for 10 minutes. Pour into a linen or cloth bag and squeeze the juice out. Return to the heating vessel, add the sugar and boil for 5 minutes. Skim, strain, bottle and cork. This is extremely good mixed with soda or water as a summer drink.

DRINKS FOR ALL SEASONS

The R. M.'S Revival

Put cracked ice in the bottom of a glass. Add ½ jigger of lemon and lime juice, 1 jigger of Jameson's whiskey and 1 teaspoon of caster sugar. Stir well and decorate with a slice of orange.

Irish Coffee

Put one teaspoon of sugar into a warmed, stemmed glass. Fill the glass threequarters full with strongish black coffee. Add two good measures of Irish whiskey. Float thick cream on the top of the liquid using the back of a spoon.

Drink the coffee through the thick layer of cream.

Bantry Beano

--------------------INGREDIENTS--------------------

1 blade mace
8 cloves
1 stick of cinnamon
1 teaspoon allspice

1 orange, quartered
2 bottles port
brandy (optional)

--------------------METHOD--------------------

Put all the spices in ½ pint (300 ml) of water and simmer gently until the liquid is reduced by half. Strain. Put the strained liquid in a larger saucepan with the orange. Add the port and heat thoroughly but on no account let it boil. If desired, add about a cocktail-glassful of brandy just before serving.

St Patrick's Penance

————————————INGREDIENTS————————————

1 tablespoon crème de menthe   1 tablespoon Irish whiskey
1 tablespoon green chartreuse   1 dash bitters

————————————METHOD————————————

Stir all the ingredients together well. Add cracked ice to chill. Strain into a 3-fl-oz (75-ml) cocktail glass.

Skibbereen Stinger

————————————INGREDIENTS————————————

1 measure of Jamaican rum   juice of half a lemon
1 teaspoon sugar   piece of cinnamon stick
2 cloves

————————————METHOD————————————

Heat a tumbler well. Put all the ingredients in together and top up with boiling water.

Clonakilty Cup

————————————INGREDIENTS————————————

juice of half a lemon   1 tablespoon rum
1 teaspoon caster sugar   1 strawberry
jigger of Irish whiskey   1 raspberry
1 tablespoon sloe gin   1 cherry

————————————METHOD————————————

Shake the liquid ingredients well with cracked ice and strain into a 5-fl-oz (150-ml) punch glass. Decorate with the fruit.

Baltimore Bomber

―――――――――――――INGREDIENTS―――――――――――――

½ Irish whiskey
¼ Royal Irish Coffee Liqueur

¼ Royal Irish Mint Chocolate
   Liqueur
Cream

―――――――――――――METHOD―――――――――――――

Stir all the ingredients, except the cream, together well. Float the cream on top.

Slipper's Surprise

―――――――――――――INGREDIENTS―――――――――――――

1 tablespoon vermouth
2 tablespoons Irish whiskey

1 dash orange bitters

―――――――――――――METHOD―――――――――――――

Stir all the ingredients together well with cracked ice and strain into a 3-fl-oz (75-ml) cocktail glass.

Drimoleague Dinger

―――――――――――――INGREDIENTS―――――――――――――

1 jigger Irish whiskey
1 tablespoon French vermouth

1 teaspoon crème de menthe

―――――――――――――METHOD―――――――――――――

Stir all the ingredients together with cracked ice and strain into a 3-fl-oz (75-ml) cocktail glass. Serve with green olives.

Mrs O'Fee's Folly

―――――――――――――INGREDIENTS―――――――――――――

1 tablespoon vermouth
2 tablespoons Irish whiskey

1 teaspoon Irish Mist
twist of lemon

―――――――――――――METHOD―――――――――――――

Stir all the liquid ingredients well with cracked ice and strain into a cocktail glass. Decorate with a twist of lemon.

Skebawn Scorcher

------------------------------INGREDIENTS------------------------------

1 teaspoon sugar
sprig of fresh mint

crushed ice
1 measure Paddy Irish whiskey

------------------------------METHOD------------------------------

In a 12-fl-oz (350-ml) glass, dissolve the sugar in a little warm water. Crush a leaf of mint in the sugary water and leave it there. Pack the glass with crushed ice. Add Paddy whiskey. Stir well. Decorate with a few pieces of mint leaf.

MRS CADOGAN'S HERBAL REMEDIES

Angelica Punch – for a cold

1 oz (25 g) of freshly gathered angelica root should be chopped up and steeped in 2 pints (1·1 litres) of brandy for 5 days. Then add 1 oz (25 g) pulped, skinned almond. Strain the liquid through a fine muslin and add 1 pint (600 ml) of liquid sugar. Bottle the mixture and take when, and as often, as required.

Aniseed Tea – relieves coughs and asthma

A half pint (300 ml) of boiling water is poured over 2 teaspoonfuls of crushed aniseed and sweetened with honey. Take 2 teaspoons four times a day.

Basil Tea – relieves obstruction in the stomach and bowel

Take a handful of green tops from the plant and infuse in boiling water. Take one tablespoonful four times a day.

Camomile Tea – sooths strain, nervousness and weariness

Infuse the leaves in boiling water or, even better, add 1 oz (25 g) of the flowers to 1 pint (600 ml) of boiling water.

Caraway Poultice – clears earache

Take a teaspoonful of bruised seeds and moisten them with alcohol. Press them over the ear with the crust of a hot new loaf.

Cayenne Pepper – relieves cases of mild frostbite

Sprinkle cayenne pepper inside the sock and on the foot. Relief is instant.

Cowslip Lotion – clears spots and blemishes

Simply boil the leaves in water. Dip a soft cloth into the lotion and rub the affected area day and night.

Dandelion Tea – aids sufferers from rheumatism

Infuse one teaspoonful of leaves in boiling water for 10 minutes. Sweeten with honey. Take twice a day.

Dill Water – improves the quality of hair and nails

Pour boiling water over a teaspoonful of seeds. Sweeten with honey. Take twice a day.

Lemon Balm Tea – relieves migraine and bad headaches

Infuse a teaspoonful of leaves in boiling water for 5 minutes, sweeten with honey, and take once every hour.

Marigold Flower – soothes a bee or wasp sting

A marigold flower rubbed onto a sting immediately relieves the swelling and the pain.

Marjoram Binding – cures a sore throat

Make marjoram tea by infusing one heaped teaspoon of marjoram with ½ pint (300 ml) of water. Soak a towel in the hot tea, and bind it around the throat (but not too tightly!).

Nettle Bunches – eases bad attacks of rheumatism

Bind freshly cut nettle plants into tight bunches and beat the affected parts. Then apply cotton cloths soaked in vinegar and keep in position for two hours. Then, with more bound nettles, once more beat the same area. Painful but highly effective.

Rose Water – soothes sore eyes

Soak fresh rose petals in warm water and then apply to the eye directly.

Rosemary Water – acts as an insect repellent

Mix a teaspoon of crushed rosemary with ½ pint (300 ml) of beer. Leave for three days and then sieve. Apply when required.

Sage Tea – cures sore throats

Infuse one teaspoon of leaves per cup in boiling water and drink immediately.

Sliced Horseradish – cures chilblains

Slice raw horseradish root and rub it morning and night on the chilblain until it goes away.

Sunflower Gin Punch – a successful cure for coughs and colds

Boil 2 oz (50 g) sunflower seeds in 2 pints (1·1 litre) of water until the liquid is reduced to 12 fl oz (350 ml). Add 6 oz (175 g) of gin and 6 oz (175 g) of sugar. Take 3 or 4 times a day in doses of one or two teaspoons.

Tansy Water – expels worms in children

1 oz (25 g) chopped tansy to 1 pint (600 ml) of boiling water, taken morning and night.

Thyme baths – soothing, scented and medicinal

Scatter some sprigs of thyme in the bath.

Vervain Necklace – reduces scrofulous conditions

Wind vervain around a string and put it round your neck. Wear it until the scrofula dies down.

Wormwood Wine – dispels indigestion

Boil up 1½ pints (0·8 litre) of water with 1 oz (25 g) of wormwood flower and bud. Leave to stand for 12 hours. Take the clear liquid in the same amount of white wine, 3 times a day.

MRS CADOGAN'S
HOUSEHOLD HINTS

Do not put the remains of a joint of meat away on a plate on which it was carved, as its juices will quickly sour and turn the meat bad.

Pork crackling crackles if you rub its skin with salt and olive oil before cooking. The loin of pork gives the best crackling as it has a thick layer of fat beneath the skin.

To prevent milk from going sour, throw a pinch of bicarbonate of soda into it. This does not alter the taste of the milk.

Hang game birds by the neck and hares by the back legs.

A large vase of marigolds absorbs kitchen smells.

Cook root vegetables with the lid on, and green vegetables with the lid off.

To keep salt dry at all times, keep a little ground arrowroot in the salt-cellar.

To prevent milk boiling over, place a pie funnel in the centre of the saucepan.

Heat your bread-knife in hot water before slicing freshly baked bread.

Food should be eaten as fresh as possible, while drink should be well matured.

Always boil cabbage with a little aniseed.

―――――――――――――――WHEN YOU'RE FEELING LOW――――――――――――

A good remedy for a cough is a new-laid egg dissolved in lemon juice, drunk straight down.

To cure a headache, squeeze half a lemon into sugarless black coffee.

Boil together nettles and dandelions for children to drink who wet their beds.

To cure mumps, put the patient under a donkey three times.

For a rash, put bay leaves on the affected area.

If you have constipation, eat an apple followed by a hot cup of tea.

To cure ringworm and shingles, make a cloth belt, strung with quicksilvers (from the back of a mirror), the white of an egg and Holy Water. Wear around the waist until the ring has gone.

To prevent cramp, sleep with a bottle cork in the bedding.

―――――――――――――――AROUND THE HOUSE――――――――――――――

Remove soot from the carpet by sprinkling salt onto it before vacuuming.

Improve the burning power of coal by adding one handful of washing soda per hundredweight of coal.

Clean a fountain pen thoroughly by soaking it in vinegar.

Vinegar removes paint stains from glass.

Peppermint oil outside a mouse-hole will drive the mice away.

To clean piano keys: a paste of boot whitener and methylated spirit applied with a pad of cotton wool, and polished with a silk cloth.

To remove candlewax from a surface, cover with layers of brown paper and press with a hot iron.

To improve the shine on shoes, squeeze a few drops of lemon juice onto the blacking brush after putting it in the polish.

Potato water removes mud stains from cloth.

Put soap in the hinges of a door, to stop it creaking.

INDEX